BRAVE
Surrender

BRAVE
Surrender

LET GOD'S LOVE
Rewrite Your Story

KIM WALKER-SMITH

ZONDERVAN®

ZONDERVAN

Brave Surrender
Copyright © 2019 by Kim Walker-Smith

Requests for information should be addressed to:
Zondervan, *3900 Sparks Dr. SE, Grand Rapids, Michigan 49546*

ISBN 978-0-310-35399-7 (softcover)

ISBN 978-0-310-35403-1 (audio)

ISBN 978-0-310-35401-7 (ebook)

Author is represented by the literary agency of The Fedd Agency, Inc., P.O. Box 341973, Austin, TX 78734.

Cover design: James W. Hall IV
Cover photo: Mary Claire Stewart
Interior design: Kait Lamphere

Printed in the United States of America

19 20 21 22 23 24 25 26 /LSC/ 15 14 13 12 11 10 9 8 7 6 5 4 3 2 1

To my children—Wyatt, Bear, and Maisie.
You give me the strength to keep fighting
for the best version of myself.
I pray that you will also find Jesus
in every hardship you face
and never forget how loved you are.

PRAISE FOR
Brave Surrender

I so love Kim's heart for worship and her passion to help others encounter the love and redemption of the Father. *Brave Surrender* is a book of beautiful truth and personal stories that will be an encouragement and inspiration to all who read it.

Kari Jobe

God had a great surprise and gift for the church when He created Kim Walker-Smith's voice. She sings with a passion and abandon unlike any other I've known. However, this kind of freedom doesn't come without struggle, without pain, or without a fight. Thank you, Kim, for being so honest and open with your story. I know this book will be a lifeline to so many in their own journey of faith.

Chris Tomlin

What most people know about Kim Walker-Smith is what they've experienced as they've heard her lead worship on an album or on stage. Countless numbers of people have been impacted by her voice and the anointing on her life. But what most may not know is the woman behind the voice—the daughter, mother, wife, friend, preacher, and leader I've been privileged to know since she was eighteen. What has most impressed me is not her ability to lead worship, but her willingness and hunger to embrace growth and allow God to shape her life. Up close and personal, I've watched her walk with Jesus off the stage. Through mountains and valleys, in hard times and good times, she has consistently positioned herself in full surrender to God. In *Brave Surrender*, Kim invites us on the same journey of intimately knowing the love of a Father who will never leave us or forsake us and calls us to trust Him completely. With raw honesty and vulnerability, Kim inspires us to experience a freedom that can only come through surrender to a Father who surrendered all for us.

Banning Liebscher, founder of Jesus Culture

Brave Surrender is a majestic telling of the unparalleled power of God's love. Kim Walker-Smith vulnerably opens up the scenes of her life, allowing us to dive into the experiences that led her to understand the splendor of surrendering to a good God. Read and know that God's all-consuming love is waiting for you.

Lisa Bevere, New York Times bestselling author

Kim Walker-Smith's book grants us a glimpse into God's work in her life. For all who seek to discover their gifts, find healing for their hearts, and minister to others, this wonderful book is a terrific resource.

Max Lucado, pastor and bestselling author

CONTENTS

Chapter 1 | HE LOVES US

It was a Friday night in July 2006—the first night of our annual Jesus Culture conference. I stood just offstage, peering out from behind a thick curtain at the people filling the auditorium. A hum of nervous anticipation coursed through me like electricity.

Our team—worship leaders Chris Quilala, Melissa How, and I, along with our band—was about to record our second live album, *We Cry Out*. This time we were filming as well. After the success of our first album, *Everything*, we couldn't wait to see what would happen with this one.

When we released *Everything*, none of us had any intention of going on to become a band and record multiple albums. Our sole purpose had been to give kids something to take home from our conferences that would help them enter into worship again. From the reports of youth leaders and kids themselves, we knew they were having amazing times of connecting to Jesus in worship at our conferences. The kids eagerly told their pastors about the ways they were experiencing God's presence and love, and their response had been consistently evident in their loud and physically expressive worship. However, when they went back to their homes and lives, it seemed they were struggling to hold on to that connection with the presence of God.

By the time they came to the next conference, we felt as though we had to help them go back and pick up again at the beginning of their journey into intimacy with the Lord. The first session usually seemed flat—the kids would all kind of stand there and stare at us like they weren't sure what to do with themselves. It seemed like there was a lot of distraction in the room, and their faces and body language clearly said they weren't really excited to worship.

As a team, we understood from our own relationships with Jesus that sometimes life (stress, work, school, and the like) can pull all our attention from that relationship. Our connection to Jesus is not a onetime thing; it is something to fight for and nourish. It was in these moments of worship that the teens developed intimacy with Jesus, and we thought it would be incredible if they had a recording of the worship to take home and help incite their hunger for more of Him.

Wonderfully, that is exactly what happened! *Everything* became a huge success—in terms of sales numbers, but also, and more importantly, in fueling kids' devotion to the Lord. We heard countless testimonies from kids who described how the moments we recorded on the album had led them into fresh encounters with Jesus and stirred their passion to keep running after Him.

Parents were emailing us to tell us how their teens were spending time praying and worshiping Jesus in their bedrooms at home. They told us that their kids insisted on listening to the CD in the car every time they had to drive somewhere, were eager to talk about Jesus, and were excited to go to church.

When we had arrived at the venue earlier in the day for the Jesus Culture conference, we were happily surprised to hear kids worshiping together outside as they waited in line to enter the building. As the first session was about to start, they rushed to the front, crowded around the stage, and were shouting praise before the first song could take off.

Even as I waited backstage, I could feel that the level of hunger for worship in the room was much greater than what I had experienced in past conferences. It was obvious that these kids didn't need to start over in worship; they were ready to go deeper than ever before! I couldn't wait to see where God would lead us and which moments of encounter with Him would be captured forever. I was convinced that *We Cry Out* would only be more powerful and bear more fruit than we had already seen.

Sloppy and Wet

There was, however, one song in the set list I was a little nervous about. It was not a typical worship song—it was very wordy and contained a phrase that our team wasn't sure the kids would really understand: *so heaven meets earth like a sloppy, wet kiss.*

The first time I heard "How He Loves" was at a church event in Fort Mill, South Carolina. I had just moved from Redding, California, to Charlotte, North Carolina, which was very close to Fort Mill. A few months before, I was feeling stuck in my relationship with God. A few friends told me that God was doing good things out there, so I made the move in hopes that something new would be awakened inside me. "How He Loves" led me into an encounter with the Lord that ignited fresh passion in my heart.

My friend John Mark McMillan had written the song after the tragic death of a friend. As he sang it, I began to feel the overwhelming love of Jesus for me. It wasn't the first time I had felt this love so strongly, but as I stood in this room full of strangers, the words of that song came alive inside me with incredible intensity. Admittedly, it was a little strange at first to sing "heaven meets earth like a sloppy, wet kiss," but as the words came out of my mouth, I realized the truth of that lyric.

When heaven shows up, when Jesus intervenes in my life, when I encounter God, it can be messy, passionate, and all-consuming. Not in a negative way, but in a way that causes me to say, "I am surrendering to Your love completely, God. I am not fighting for control, and I am trusting You in every outcome." And when Jesus shows up, He covers *everything*, just like a sloppy, wet kiss.

I felt totally convicted that Jesus loves me regardless of any mistakes I've made, my past, or what anybody says about me. *He loves me.* I sobbed through the entire song. It felt as though a wildfire was sweeping through my heart. Then suddenly, I was consumed with one burning thought: *Everybody needs to encounter this love! Everybody needs to know this love!*

I wanted to shout it from the mountaintops. *Isn't this the question everybody asks?* I thought to myself. *Am I loved? Does God really love me?* I felt like the girl in the classroom, raising her hand and shouting, "Ooooh, pick me, pick me! I know the answer!" I wanted to find a way to tell everyone.

When I moved back to Redding, California, and the band asked me which songs I would like to lead for our second album, I knew immediately that I wanted to sing "How He Loves." It took a little convincing, but in the end, I won them over. As for winning over our audience—all I knew was that if they experienced what *I* had experienced through this song, they would love it as much as I did. For this reason, I desperately wanted my version of "How He Loves" to be *awesome*. I wanted everyone in the room to experience love like a sloppy, wet kiss that covers everything and melts our hearts into total surrender.

On that Friday night at the conference, Banning Liebscher, director of Jesus Culture, finally gave us the go-ahead nod—it was time to start. I took a deep breath, stepped out from behind the curtain, and walked onstage.

As the band launched into the first song, I felt my nerves give way to the comfort, familiarity, and pure enjoyment of doing what I was made to do. I *love* to worship Jesus. I cannot contain the joy I feel when I sense His presence moving in the room.

As I always do when I'm singing, I focused intently on every single word coming out of my mouth, feeling total conviction in the truth of each lyric. I could sense the way these declarations were bringing us deeper and deeper into God's presence. Spread before me, I saw a sea of faces looking heavenward, tears streaming down cheeks, arms reaching up. I heard an army of voices singing at the top of their lungs. As I looked out over the crowd that night, I knew with absolute certainty that these people would not leave the room the same. At the same time, my heart began to pound with the hope and expectation that the Lord was about to do something new.

"How He Loves" was the last song in our set, and when we finally reached it, I could feel the atmosphere change in the room. The presence of the Holy Spirit became as tangible as the nose on my face. I could feel His love filling the room like a heavy, warm blanket.

At the same time, something powerful was happening, and I began scrambling in my head to find the words to describe it.

It was as if God had decided in this precious moment to tear down every lie that says He can't love us. Lies that say, "You are a mistake. How could anyone love a mistake?" Lies that convince you that you've made too much of a mess of your life for Jesus ever to love you, that you aren't worthy of forgiveness.

These lies and many more were being demolished by the love of God. Every line of the song was like a sledgehammer smashing a wall. As we sang, "He loves us, oh how He loves us," shame was relinquishing its hold on hearts; fear was being swallowed up in an ocean of grace; and we were finally believing the truth that had always been there: *He loves us!*

The whole atmosphere in the room changed. Where earlier it felt like I was pressing up against a wall, I felt like now I was running freely down a hill. Leading everyone in singing the chorus was effortless, as every voice was shouting out the words. The little hairs on my arm were standing up, as I felt the tingly sensation of something happening—something beyond my natural abilities to manufacture.

This is the kind of moment in a worship set that I live for. I am no longer a leader, but instead I am simply a sister and daughter enjoying the presence of her Father with those around her. I feel my whole body settle into a calm and surrender as Jesus walks into the room and does what only He can do. It's the moment when it is no longer about a song, or a schedule, or a routine. It is plainly just about Jesus touching His people.

After a few minutes, we reached a lull in the song. I desperately wanted to put words to what was happening in the room. It was urgent that not a single person miss the freedom God was offering. I reached for words, notes, a melody, a phrase— anything that might define this encounter. And what came out of me was a blur of . . . something. The phrases coming out of my mouth sounded disjointed and awkward to my ears:

> *And right now, if you haven't encountered the love of God—and you would KNOW, because you would never be the same . . . you would never be the same AGAIN!—And if you, if you want to encounter the love of God right now, you better just BRACE yourself! Because He's about to just BLOW in this place! And WE'RE GOING TO ENCOUNTER THE LOVE OF GOD!*

I could feel heat radiating from my cheeks as I finished speaking, but there was nothing I could do except plunge ahead and finish the song and the rest of the set. As Banning came out to pray and wrap up our time of worship, disappointment and frustration began to churn inside me. I slipped offstage after Banning's "Amen" and felt tears welling up in my eyes. My head was a jumble of embarrassed thoughts: *Oh, Kim, you missed that one. Way to ruin the moment and sound like a bumbling idiot. Talk about sloppy and wet—that was beyond sloppy. You were probably singing off-key too. Everyone's going to be disappointed.*

Then I remembered the worst thing of all: *it's all on tape.*

Wiping my eyes, I looked around frantically for Banning. I spotted him and hurried over, desperate to prevent the disaster I was imagining.

"Hey—" I began.

"That was awesome!" Banning interrupted.

"Um, thanks," I said. "Hey, can we please cut out that part where I talked in 'How He Loves'? It just felt really awkward. I was stumbling over the words, and I'm sure it didn't come out very well."

Banning laughed. It was the laugh of a dad laughing at his child because he thinks she is cute. "No, it was *so* good!" he insisted. "It was my favorite part—it was so powerful!"

This was not what I wanted to hear. "Banning, *please!*" I said, trying not to freak out completely. "If you care about me at all, do *not* put that on the recording! I'm serious! It was so . . . so bad! I don't even think people were singing or connecting to the song at all!"

Nothing I said made the grin on Banning's face budge an inch. He stubbornly maintained that my embarrassing moment had been the best part of the whole night and that all of the awkwardness was in my head. But nothing he said changed my mind either. All his assurances did was convince me that he really was acting like a dad, because only a dad would think a performance like that was good. Only a dad could look at a scribble on a paper, tell you it was a beautiful self-portrait, and pin it to the fridge.

I walked away, plotting how I was going to convince him not to ruin my life by putting it on the final cut.

The YouTube Effect

In the end, despite multiple and increasingly desperate attempts, I failed to convince Banning to withhold that moment from the album. The day *We Cry Out* was released, I felt incredibly raw, exposed, and vulnerable. I felt like I had recorded myself reading my diary and then blasted it out for the whole world to hear. I braced myself for the teasing, criticism, and mocking that I felt certain would come.

Sure enough, as the days rolled on, reactions to the song began to pile up. But they weren't the responses I had expected.

I remember sitting in a café a couple of weeks after the album released and suddenly hearing "Kiiimmm!" from across the room. Stunned, I turned to see my friend Sarah running up to me, apparently about to burst with excitement. "I have not stopped listening to your new album!" she exclaimed, her eyes shining. "I have never felt the love of God like I do when I'm listening to 'How He Loves.' I've had it on repeat for days!"

Other friends found me after church to describe, with similar intensity, the impact the album was having on them. Person after person said they could feel God's tangible love filling the room and shaking them to the core. Some had cried for days as God delivered them from shame. They were experiencing freedom as old mind-sets suddenly shifted and negative thoughts and lies were replaced with truth, love, joy, and peace. Where a weight or a burden had been holding them down, now they felt lightheartedness and a deeper trust in Jesus.

Soon, random strangers at church began stopping to tell me the same thing, their voices full of passion as they described the love they had encountered. The majority of them mentioned that the part where I was speaking was especially powerful.

I couldn't help but continue to be baffled that these were the testimonies coming out of that crazy moment. Yes, I was glad that people were encountering God's love—that was exactly what I had hoped and prayed for. Yet no matter how many times I thought about (or worse, heard) that moment on the album, I felt nothing but embarrassment and a hope that people would soon delete the song from their playlists.

Nothing could have prepared me for what was about to happen next.

A month or two after the release of *We Cry Out*, my younger brother, Matt, who was about fifteen years old at the time, called me. "Kim," he said excitedly, "you're on YouTube!"

"What is YouTube?" I asked, bewildered.

He told me to get online and guided me to a web page where I saw the video of me singing "How He Loves." My stomach dropped to the floor, and embarrassment flooded through me once again. *NO WAY.* This vulnerable moment of mine was floating around in cyberspace for the whole world to see? I was suddenly possessed by the urge to mysteriously disappear from planet Earth.

Then I saw the number posted below the video: 20,347.

"Matt," I shouted through the phone, "what is this number underneath the video?"

"That's the number of views this video has had."

Kill me, I thought. *I'm dead. I have to change my name.*

That number was ringing through my head. I got off the phone and immediately called Banning.

"Banning," I shrieked. "I'm dying!"

"What's going on?"

"Did you know that someone put 'How He Loves' on this thing called YouTube, and it's been seen more than twenty thousand times?" My voice rose to a scream.

"Yes!" Banning exclaimed excitedly. "Isn't it amazing?"

I was speechless. I could only think that I was living in some alternate universe where your worst nightmares not only become reality but are then broadcast across the internet. As I was pondering the cost of a new identity, I heard Banning say, "We're working to get it taken down, but then we'll put it right back up again so it's there legally."

Oh great, I thought. As he had for the umpteenth time by now, Banning tried to calm me down and assure me that the video was a powerful moment and that God was up to something spectacular here. Despite the positive feedback we had gotten so far, however, I was sure Banning was being way too optimistic.

I drove home from work that day, went straight to my room, and lay down on my bed. My heart was pounding, and tears stung my eyes. I just could not believe what was happening. Thousands of people had seen me in a moment I wished I could have erased from history. Many had watched that moment *over and over*. Instead of fading from the scene, "How He Loves" was on its way to massive exposure—and so was I. That meant I was either facing embarrassment of epic proportions—or . . .

Or God had a plan.

I began to feel the gentle presence of Jesus surrounding me as I lay on my bed. I could feel the love of my Father—a love I have come to know very well—filling up my insides and causing the wind and the waves of my stormy emotions to calm.

After a few moments of simply receiving His love and peace, I sensed the Holy Spirit gently beginning to help me understand how I had come to be in this place. He first reminded me of a prayer I had prayed many times. I had prayed it long before I ever heard John Mark's beautiful song. I had prayed it in desperation: *God, help me to love like You love.*

This prayer had been born out of a journey of healing I had walked through several years earlier. As you'll learn in the coming chapters, things I had experienced in my childhood had led me to become a woman full of wounds, scars, pain, anger, fear, hatred, and deep sorrow. Finally, through God's insistent wooing in my life, I reached the place where I was desperate to be free. I became convinced that if I could come to know His love in a radical way and see my life through His eyes, then I would view my past and those who brought me pain through the lens of that love. Surely, that was the way I could forgive them, love them, and love myself, for "we love because he first loved us" (1 John 4:19).

Sure enough, all of that turned out to be true. God had met me with His love in a series of profound healing encounters that utterly transformed me. On the other side of those encounters, all I wanted was to live in that love and share it with others. My daily prayer became, "God, help me to love like You love." His presence became the air I breathed. I could feel His heart for people in a way I never had before. I could feel the heart of a Father calling out to His prodigal child to come home. I could feel the heart of a Mother, a love that never, ever gives up on her child and always believes the best. I could feel the heart of a Brother, who swears, "Come hell or high water, I will not forsake you."

It was *this* love I had felt when I first heard "How He Loves." That experience hadn't just been about me receiving love from Jesus; it had been about me being consumed by the desire to help *others* receive it. This was why I had said, "Pick me!" And even though my version of the song hadn't gone the way I had envisioned, I had to admit that the results I was seeing were exactly what I had wanted. People were receiving God's love.

More peace flooded through me as I lay on my bed and finally understood that God had had a plan all along. That plan had started before the recording, before I heard the song, before my healing, and even before the song was written. It was not about me. It didn't matter that I was embarrassed or felt foolish. It didn't matter that I was terrified of what people thought. The only thing that mattered was a Father wanting more than anything for His children to know His love for them.

But it *was* about me in one sense, I realized. This was another opportunity for me to surrender.

Before my healing encounters with the love of God, I knew that I needed His love and that His love would transform me. What I didn't know was that letting God love me would require me to make one of the riskiest and most vulnerable and courageous decisions I had ever made—the decision to surrender. I had to let Him love me on His terms, and that meant letting go of the questions, demands, and needs I had been insisting He address. It would be a long journey of learning ahead.

Now I was in another moment where I needed to surrender. I had to let go of the way I wished that vulnerable moment on stage had gone. I didn't get to bury it or go back and turn it into something polished and articulate. I had to let it be what it was and let God use it the way He wanted to.

Brave Enough to Surrender

Over the last ten years, I've had to continue to surrender that moment to the Lord. I know it's probably surprising to everyone but me, but to this day, I still have times when I wish I could have convinced Banning to switch out the live track of "How He Loves" with a perfectly produced studio version featuring *no* talking, and to leave the video off *We Cry Out* entirely.

That would have saved me from experiences I could have lived without—like event chauffeurs loudly quoting my entire speech from the song while taking me to a concert venue or reluctantly listening as random people at the grocery store want to quote it to me, complete with hand motions.

Yet I am also fully aware of the reality that this recording is the catalyst God has used to bring me to where I am today and to bring countless people into transforming encounters with Him. It has arguably been the recording that brought significant exposure to Jesus Culture and helped launch it into the movement it has become.

Today, that YouTube video has more than 20 million views. For ten years, I have received a regular stream of emails and social media comments from people who are watching it for the first time, letting me know about how Jesus is showing them His love. It would take another book to record all the stories and testimonies of what a single moment caught on a recording has meant to so many, but I'll mention just a few.

One email came from a woman who told me she was in a lesbian relationship. Someone had emailed her the link to the video. After she watched it, she kept playing it over and over. She couldn't stop thinking about Jesus. In her email, she asked me if I thought Jesus could possibly love her in the way I was singing about. It wrecked me. I was happy to share the love of God with her.

I have received multiple emails from mothers who sent the video to their teenage children who had wandered from the Lord. They each reported that their kids had ended up in a sobbing heap on the floor, experiencing the love of a Father for the first time.

The parents of a very young boy who was battling cancer in a Ronald McDonald House in San Francisco wrote to tell me that their son's favorite song was "How He Loves." He asked his mom to play it over and over. My husband and I went to visit him. I sang the song to him and watched as pure joy and peace came over his face and his parents' faces. He went to live with Jesus a few weeks after that.

The more I have seen the way God has used and continues to use this song to bring people into an encounter with His love, the more I have gained His perspective on it. I now know that God hasn't used it in spite of my raw, awkward vulnerability but *because* of it. When I push my embarrassed feelings aside and look at what actually happened in that moment, I see my true self—a woman who has been radically transformed by encountering God's love and who lives to invite others into the same experience.

There was no way I could hide, control, or perfect the way I expressed my hunger for people to know God's love in that moment. It was raw, but most important, it was *real*. And only because this was the true, deep cry of my heart could it resonate with the heart cries of those who heard it and immediately knew, "*Yes*, that is what I want to say!" As those genuine cries rose to heaven, Jesus responded from His heart for us.

In that awkward moment in the middle of the song, I said, "We're never the same after we've encountered the love of God." It is very common for a Christian to say that Jesus loves them. We learn this in Sunday school. We sing about it in our songs. We memorize it in Scripture. But until we experience this truth in a tangible way, it won't become a deep conviction we live by. My husband can tell me he loves me all day long, but unless he actually puts those words into action and shows me his love for me, it's hard to believe and even harder to respond to.

I know that Jesus loves me because I have felt it, heard it, and seen it with my own eyes. It is that experience of His love that provokes radical change in me. And ever since I've encountered His love, this is the conviction that drives my worship: *I don't want to just say that Jesus loves me; I want to know it deep down inside and be changed by it.*

If you've ever encountered the love of God, then you already know what I've discovered: a love encounter, by its very nature, only happens through a courageous and vulnerable act of surrender. To receive God's love, we must *let* Him love us. We must abandon every effort to keep Him at a distance or every effort to control the way He touches and transforms us. We have to let Him come close—into the deepest parts of who we are—and change everything with His love.

I'm convinced there can be no relationship with Him without this brave surrender. Sometimes I feel like a broken record—constantly encouraging people to surrender their lives, lay down their questions and accusations, and let down their walls. I look for many ways to tell people what I desperately do not want them to miss: *God loves you so much, and when you experience that, you will never be the same.*

I tell them that I know what it's like to struggle to trust Jesus when bad things happen—to let go of all the pain and fear, the unanswered questions, and the powerful urge to be in control, and to let God be God in their lives. And I tell them who I've discovered this God to be—a Father who loves with a love that can't be earned, never gives up, and meets us right where we are, no matter the mess or the storm in which we find ourselves.

With everything in me, I try to give them the courage to fall into His arms.

But of course, I can only tell people so much in one worship set, conference session talk, or interview. This is why I've decided to tell the whole story of how I have come to know these things about God's love. I've decided to step into another moment of raw vulnerability and invite you, and anyone who reads this book, to share it with me—all because I want you to believe me and to believe Him. *He loves you with a love that cannot be measured, stopped, or contained!*

Chapter 2

SAFETY SHATTERED

If there's one thing I know without question, it's that one moment can change your whole life. Just as there are moments that heal, restore, and revive, there are also moments that shatter, wound, and destroy.

The first of these shattering moments in my life occurred when I was two years old. My dad was riding his motorcycle home one day when a woman in a car ran a stop sign at an intersection and struck him. He flew through the air and hit his head on the pavement very hard (he wasn't wearing a helmet). At the hospital, the doctors told my mom he had sustained a very serious brain injury and was in a coma. They couldn't be sure he would wake up, and if he did, he was unlikely to regain full functionality.

My mom took me to visit my dad at the hospital. Having no concept that he was unconscious, I began talking to him. I'm sure it was mostly baby gibberish, but I don't doubt for a second that I talked a lot (a trait I still possess). As I began talking, his body began to move, as though he was responding to the sound of my voice. The doctors were intrigued by this and told my mom to bring me around more in case the sound of my voice might call him back to consciousness.

Much to the doctors' surprise, after ten days in a coma, my dad woke up. Even more amazingly, he learned to walk and talk again. It wasn't easy, but with a lot of therapy, he got there. However, those weren't the only difficulties he had to overcome. When a person suffers a brain injury that severe, there are levels of healing the brain goes through as it learns to function again. His speech was a little different; his memory really suffered; and he struggled to do simple tasks, like pour himself a glass of iced tea. He had moments of rage and sporadic yelling, as well as moments when he acted silly and childlike—all typical stages, we learned, of his brain trying to get its wires firing somewhat normally.

As a little girl, I could never understand why my parents divorced two years after the accident. Now as an adult, I can imagine what a strain it must have been on their marriage. They were both young. My mom was twenty-one and pregnant with my younger sister when the accident happened, and it couldn't have been easy trying to raise a toddler and a newborn while her husband worked to relearn basic cognitive, verbal, and motor skills. Their marriage just couldn't recover from the trauma of it all.

My mom, sister, and I went to live with my grandparents. I can remember feeling confused as to why Mommy and Daddy weren't living in the same house and also irritated when we had to work out "who has the kids on what weekend." I remember feeling sad and scared when they fought.

My mom gave me an old wedding picture of them lacquered on a piece of wood with felt on the back. I used to sleep with it under my pillow, and at night I would hold it and cry. I was angry about the motorcycle wreck and angry that they had divorced. I was convinced that if the wreck hadn't happened, they would still be married.

Stepfather #1

Within a year of my parents' divorce, my mom married my first stepfather, Peter. We moved in with him, and I began kindergarten. I don't remember where Peter worked or the sound of his voice, but I have never forgotten the way he looked at me—with intense hatred and contempt. He had an office in our house where he would work occasionally. To a little girl who loved art, the paper, pens, and colored pencils in the office made it seem like a room of treasures. Peter would let my little sister come in and draw on paper, but he made me sit in the doorway and just watch. He always showed favor to her and anger toward me. I felt very rejected and confused. Hatred was not even an emotion I knew or could communicate at that point in my life—all I knew was that I could feel it, and it hurt.

My mom was married to Peter for only about a year, and most of that time has been blacked out in my memory. As a teen, I had a recurring nightmare about him in which I'm playing with my sister in our room, and we decide to call our mom because we want something. Hearing no response, we begin to walk through the house looking for her, but she is nowhere to be found. Then we go to her room and find the door shut. As I reach up to the doorknob to open the door, a feeling of fear and dread comes over me. My sister grabs my hand and moves behind me, as if she feels the same fear. I call out to my mom and still get no answer.

We walk slowly around the corner to the master bathroom. The door is open, and through a cloud of steam we see Peter. He looks at us with a strange look on his face and begins to walk slowly toward us. I step in front of my sister and suddenly wake up. When I wake up, I'm terrified and very upset.

After Peter and my mom split up, we went back to living with my grandparents. I adored my papa and grandma (and still do). They were strong Christians and always took us to church. Papa taught a Sunday school class for senior citizens, and my sister and I loved to tag along. We happily ate cinnamon rolls and suffered pinched cheeks, kisses, and hugs from doting old people as clouds of old cologne and perfume billowed around us. Many of them carried candies in their pockets and purses and snuck them into our little hands. If you had asked me when I was a young child if I was a Christian, I would have told you, "Yes." But as special and impactful as those moments were, church was still a ritual and not necessarily something real and understood in my life.

Grandma loved to cook, and she often baked pies. She let us eat pie for breakfast "because it has fruit in it." I often asked Papa to let me count the wrinkles on his bald head. He would scrunch up his eyebrows and lean down while I squished each wrinkle with my little fingers and counted. Even though our legs were starting to dangle far over the edge of their rockers, we loved to crawl up into their laps in the evening and let them rock us. Grandma always made a funny sound with her mouth in rhythm with the rocker, and I often fell asleep trying to mimic the sound. When we struggled to sleep at night, Papa came in and rubbed our heads and sang to us until we dozed off.

My sister and I saw our dad every other weekend and

typically spent the time doing something adventurous like fishing, camping, riding a four-wheeler, or even going to rodeos or the circus. I think my dad was trying to earn our love and was worried that we'd forget about him. It was difficult for two little girls to navigate a relationship with Dad without Mom around, but we did our best.

During one of these weekends with my dad, I remember having a conversation with him about whether he would have more kids. He said probably not. Then I asked him if he wished he had had a boy. He said that yes, he would have liked to have a boy, but he didn't get one. Somehow in my young mind, I took this as my dad saying he was disappointed that I was a girl.

From this point on, an idea began to grow in the back of my mind—the idea that because I hadn't come out as a boy like he wanted, I was a mistake. I tried to fix this by becoming a tomboy—something my dad often encouraged. He gave me pocketknives for my birthday every year, and when he took us fishing, I forced myself not to flinch when we cleaned out the fish I had caught for supper. I refused to wear dresses and ripped anything lacy off my clothing. In my mind, everything that seemed like something a boy would naturally do was somehow better than what I would do as a girl.

Stepfather #2

Toward the end of my first-grade year, my mom married my second stepdad, Greg. When Greg's job transferred him to a coastal town in Oregon, we all moved into an apartment right across the street from the beach. Though I was scared to leave my grandparents and my dad and be somewhere new, I loved living by the ocean.

Not long after we moved there, I witnessed Greg throw something across the room in a fit of rage. I had seen him get angry and shout, but it was the first time I had seen an adult become violent. It was terrifying—and it was also only the beginning of the fear he would bring into our home.

I was devastated at the end of second grade when my mom told me we'd be moving from the coastal town to the small farming town of Klamath Falls, Oregon. I didn't want to leave the ocean, start over again in a new school, and move farther away from my grandparents.

The one bright spot in the year was the arrival of our new baby brother, Matt. I was completely smitten with him, and being nine years older, I quickly took up the role of being his second mom. I loved to take care of him. When he cried at night, I would go get him, bring him into my bed, and cuddle with him until he fell asleep. I was happy to help feed him and change his diaper. However, my nurturing role also included a growing sense of protective vigilance over both my siblings, as Greg grew angrier and more volatile.

The first time I remember being hit by Greg, we had driven out to a lake for the day to swim. On the way home, I got carsick in the back seat. The windows were rolled down, and we were driving by mint fields. The smell of mint was so strong in the car that I could taste it, and it was making me more nauseous. I started complaining that I was going to be sick. After a few minutes, I guess Greg got tired of my complaining because he whipped around, slapped me across the face, and yelled, "Shut up!" My head spun, pain and shock adding to the nausea. I had never had anyone treat me like that before. To this day, I despise the smell of mint.

From that point on, I walked around on eggshells, unsure of when Greg would blow up or what would set him off. I don't remember feeling any attachment or connection to him, only a feeling of being on thin ice. School felt like an escape from the uncertainty at home. I was lucky to stay at the same school for fourth grade, and I even got to have the same teacher I had had in third grade. Her name was Mrs. Chamberlain, and I adored her. She was an artist who instilled in me a love for all things creative and the permission I needed to live outside the box. She taught me that sometimes it's okay to color outside the lines, and if learning math with pictures was easier than numbers, then so be it.

At home, the cruel behavior and the anger continued to escalate until they occurred almost daily. Greg got mad at us for fighting, and he'd hit or shove us. Dinnertime became scary and hard. We had to sit at the table in silence and eat all our food. If we didn't ask for food to be passed to us correctly, we might go hungry. If we didn't ask, "Can I be excused from the table, please?" we might be slapped. I wanted to get everything perfect so I wouldn't get in trouble, but most of the time I lost my appetite.

Greg and my mom began fighting more and more. He would come home from work, take her back to the bedroom, lock the door, and keep her in there for hours. When she finally came out, she looked very upset and tired. I was pretty sure something bad was happening in there, and I was furious. I would stand outside the door, knocking, asking to come in, saying that I needed my mom for something, and Greg would yell at me to go away. Sometimes he got mad enough to stomp over to the door, fling it open, pick me up by my neck, and throw me down.

We moved to a different house and school district the summer before fifth grade. My grandparents came to visit us at our new house that summer. It was extremely hot outside. Our new house was a manufactured house on an undeveloped lot, so there was no grass, bushes, trees, or shade. Greg sent us outside and locked the doors. At first, we were happy playing, but after a few hours, we got sweaty, thirsty, and overheated. My lips felt swollen and chapped. We begged Greg to let us come inside and get a drink of water, but he refused. We started crying, pleading with him through the window, but it was no use. My grandparents finally couldn't take it anymore. They loaded us into their car and drove us to the public swimming pool. After that, my grandma purchased an 800 number so my sister and I could call her for free from anywhere. I memorized that number.

I was miserable at my new school. I was shy when it came to making new friends, and I was struggling with the cruel way I was being treated at home. Apparently, someone noticed the signs of my struggle, because I was put in a counseling group at school with a few other girls. We played games and talked about our emotions, but I never wanted to talk about what was happening at home.

My mom and Greg started taking us to a church. In my mind, this was part of some unspoken ritual of life. If you're a good family, you go to church. My mom was the one who pushed for this, as she was raised in church and wanted all of us to participate in various church activities. I joined a girls' class on Wednesday nights. I quickly came to love and trust my teacher, so one night after all the other girls left, I went to her, took a deep breath, and told her that my stepdad was hurting me. I showed her a couple of bruises on my body and through tears explained that he was very angry and hitting me. She looked stunned and unsure of how to respond. I don't remember her saying much of anything except that she was sure "it will all be okay" and that she would pray for me.

I felt confused by her reaction. In the depths of my being, I knew that what was happening to me was not okay. I also knew that a loving adult should not stand for that kind of behavior. I had expected her to do something to help me. When she didn't, I felt hurt and sad, like she had let me down. Because I loved her so much, I convinced myself that she must have been scared, just like me. I knew it wasn't the right reaction, but it stirred something inside me that said, *If no one else will be the adult and the protector here, I must.* This moment caused me to walk further away from childhood and take on the responsibility and role of protector with my siblings and mother.

One Sunday, my mom left early to go to choir practice at church. I woke up feeling sick to my stomach, so I told Greg that I didn't think I could go to church. He ignored me and continued making breakfast, soon setting a giant pancake the size of the dinner plate in front of me. I told him I wasn't hungry and repeated that I was going to be sick. He got angry and told me to eat what he had given me. He sat next to me at the table and forced me to eat every single bite of that giant pancake, each of which I threw up after gagging it down.

After breakfast, he put me in the car with my siblings and drove us to church. When we got there, I could barely walk because I was so sick and weak from throwing up. Greg opened the janitor's closet next to the women's bathroom, put me on the floor, and walked away, shutting the door behind him. I just lay there in the dark, too weak to move or even cry. After what felt like hours, the door swung open to reveal my mom. She seemed very upset and panicked, as if she had been looking for me. She picked me up, felt my head, said I had a fever, and then rushed me home to take care of me.

Greg had children from a previous marriage who were close to my age and who lived with us off and on. One time I was wrestling with my stepsiblings, and I picked up my baby brother's plastic T-ball bat and playfully bonked one of them on the head with it. My stepsibling didn't like it and ran to tell Greg what I had done. I heard him stomping down the hallway and knew it was not going to be good. He got in my face and yelled, "Did you hit your sibling with the bat?" I tried to explain that we were all playing and wrestling and it wasn't meant to be mean or hurt anyone, but he wasn't buying it. He leaned over to pick up the bat. Knowing what was coming, I turned to run, only to find myself trapped by a chair right behind me. I jumped into the chair and curled up into a ball, sobbing, while Greg hit me with the bat. He only dropped it when my mom came running out and asked what had happened. I could barely talk from choking on my tears.

An End in Sight

After enduring years of Greg's mistreatment of me, a new emotion began to rise in me—anger. I was done. I was done walking on eggshells. I was not going to be picked up by my neck anymore. I was not going to be hit or thrown into a wall anymore.

I was not going to live in fear anymore. I'd had enough. For a long time, whenever he went on a rampage, I hid my sister and my baby brother and put myself in front of him or provoked him so he would take it out on me.

One time I had even taken a bunch of knives from the kitchen and hid them around the house while Mom and Greg were gone, convinced that at some point soon, he would try to kill me. But as the anger grew in me, I began to fight back. One time I got so angry that I charged at him and went flying through the air to attack him. With one big swoop of his arm, he blocked me and slammed me against the wall. I can't remember feeling any pain from the shove, only frustration that I hadn't succeeded. He walked away like nothing had happened, and I just lay there thinking about what I would do differently next time.

I called my grandma with increasing frequency. "That's it," I would tell her. "I've had enough! I'm calling the abuse hotline!" I had found a phone number at school for kids to call if they were being abused and always carried it in my pocket. Each time, my grandma cried and begged me not to do it, explaining that if I called, Child Protective Services would come in and remove us from the home. They might separate us, and it would likely be a little while before we were back with our mom. Then I would start sobbing because I felt so hopeless. I never wanted to be separated from my siblings, because I felt obligated to protect them. I didn't want to leave my mom for the same reason. These calls always ended with both Grandma and Papa in tears and unsure of what to do.

The beginning of the end finally came one night when my mom and Greg were having a terrible fight. Mom told me to load my siblings in the car so she could drive us to a friend's house. I had a horrible feeling in my gut, and I didn't want to leave my mom in the house alone with Greg. I walked to the door, opened it, and then shut it, making it sound like we had gone outside. Then I sat my brother and sister down by the door and motioned for them to be quiet as I crept down the hallway toward the living room. Suddenly I heard Greg say to my mom, "If you come back here, I will blow your head off!" I screamed, rushed into the living room, and jumped in front of my mom, shrieking, "I'm going to kill you!" at the top of my lungs. Mom, upset that we had heard what he had said, grabbed me and my siblings and ran out the door.

Soon after that incident, Greg began working out of town— and one day he didn't come home. I asked my mom repeatedly if he was coming back, and every time she said no. I was relieved but also terrified. I just wanted to get out of that house as soon as possible in case he changed his mind.

Greg left during the harshest winter we had experienced in Klamath Falls. School was closed for weeks (much to my delight), and we didn't see pavement for months. The snowplows couldn't keep up, and the wind created snowdrifts up to our roof, causing us to have to dig our way out of the house.

One evening we came home, and as we stepped through the door, I gasped: It was freezing cold. I could see my breath in the house. I looked at my mom, and she burst into tears. We soon discovered that none of the lights turned on. My mom walked to the refrigerator and cried even harder. When I asked her what was going on, she said she didn't have enough money to pay the bills, and now the power had been shut off. She was crying because there was nothing in the house to eat for dinner, and she didn't have any money to buy food. I begged her to take us to Grandma's. I wanted us to go live there again anyway. Instead, she loaded us up in the car, and we went to a friend's house to spend the night.

Thankfully, Grandma and Papa sent my mom some money to pay the bills and buy food. Shortly after, we moved into a little duplex. The floor in the bathroom was so rotten that mushrooms grew out of it, and the whole place was infested with giant spiders (to this day I'm deathly afraid of spiders) and mice. My mom was terrified of mice, so I had to empty the traps for her every day. But it was all my mom—now a single mother—could afford.

The following summer and year were very hard. I stayed at home through the summer, watching my sister and brother while my mom worked. One day at lunch, there was nothing but a can of green beans to eat, and my brother, sister, and I all shared it for lunch. I wanted to talk about what we had just endured, but my mom wasn't ready. I still lived with fear that Greg would show up again, but as the days passed with no sight of him, I gradually began to relax in the hope that, poor as we were, at least we were finally safe from the man who had brought so much fear and torment into our lives.

Chapter 3 | # CHURCH GIRL, INTERRUPTED

The summer before my sixth-grade year, my mom sent my sister and me to a church camp. I'm sure she, as a single mom, needed something for us to do in the summer while she was working. The church we chose was one we had only visited a few times. My mom had some friends who attended there, but Amy and I knew nobody. We were so nervous to be around new kids, and our anxiety doubled when we got to the camp and had our first charismatic church camp experience. Up to this point, my church experience had been more conservative. When my grandparents took us to church, we sang out of hymnals, listened to a choir, and sat on a pew.

I had once been to something called "camp meeting." At camp meeting, the kids were sent to fun classes that were very similar to Sunday school. Every now and then, I caught a glimpse into the Great Hall where the adults were meeting. It was much livelier then the regular Sunday morning services! Ladies were dancing with colored flags and tambourines; men were praying in a strange language; and people were falling over when someone would lay a hand on them in prayer.

These experiences taught me the little I knew about God. I understood that we prayed to Him and that He created the earth, but He often seemed to be more of a distant concept or idea that I couldn't fully wrap my little brain around. I knew about Jesus because He was the man who brought me to tears every Easter during my grandparents' church production. As an actor with long brown hair came down the aisle carrying a cross, bleeding from having been whipped by Roman guards, I would bury my face in one of my grandparents' shoulders and tearfully ask why they were hurting that man. I wanted them to stop. I don't remember hearing about Holy Spirit or understanding the Trinity at this church.

Suffice to say, my experiences up to that point had little in common with what I encountered at this camp. The first night, there was a meeting that began with worship and ended with a worship leader coming back onto the small wooden stage and playing a few songs on the piano. The speaker invited anyone who wanted to ask Jesus into their heart or receive prayer to come to the front. Other camp counselors and leaders stood waiting at the front to pray with those who came forward. Amy and I watched as kids flocked to the front, lifted their hands, cried, and prayed. Some of them fell over and began to speak in some kind of gibberish when one of the adults touched them.

Amy and I thought these people were so weird! We had never seen a church service quite like this before, especially one with children. When we learned that such services were planned for each evening of the camp, we decided to play hooky. When ministry time started the next evening, we snuck out the back and headed to our cabin to wait it out, and we returned in time for the end of the service when the candy shop opened.

We continued this pattern throughout the week. But by the last night of the camp, something was different. We made our usual move and snuck out the back to retreat to our cabin. But when we got there, this time we sat in silence. I felt a strong pulling inside me, and I was trying to figure out exactly what it was. I finally decided it was desire, tinged with jealousy. These strange kids had something I didn't have. I didn't know what to call it, but I wanted it too.

I looked up at my sister, who to my surprise was already looking at me. I recognized in her eyes the same emotion I was feeling.

"I want to go back," I said. "I don't know what those kids have, but I want it. But I'm kind of scared."

"Me too!" Amy said.

"I'll go if you go with me."

She nodded. Holding hands, we got up and walked back to the meeting hall. I could feel my heart racing and my hands trembling. Then I spotted our cabin counselor and headed toward her. When I reached her, I opened my mouth to speak. To my shock, I burst into tears.

"I don't know what these kids have, but I want it too," I said again, this time choking on the words in between sobs.

"Me too!" Amy shouted.

The counselor laughed and lifted her hand to touch me and pray. Before her hand ever made it there, I felt a warm wind blow over me. It caused me to swoop around and fall over on my side. My sister fell on top of me, and we both started speaking in a strange language, just like we had seen other kids do. I didn't do anything to make it happen—it just came out of me as I surrendered to Jesus. I could hear myself and had no idea what was happening, why I was doing it, or what I was saying. The only thing I knew was that I was encountering God. My body was tingling, and I felt a rush of excitement as a new kind of love and freedom pierced my heart. Something deep inside my soul was crying, "This is why I am alive!"

When I opened my eyes, I felt new, clean, and loved in a way I had never known. An urge to express my love to Jesus rose in me. The counselor and another woman were sitting right there praying for us, so I asked them what happened and what it was.

"Honey, that was the Holy Ghost!" said the counselor. "He filled you up, and you spoke in tongues!"

She then explained to me what "tongues" was, telling me that God had given me a heavenly language as a gift and that I could use it to pray, praise, and give thanks to Him. She said that sometimes God might give me or someone else an interpretation of what I was saying, and sometimes He would not (see 1 Corinthians 14). I felt pretty special to have a prayer language all my own, and I couldn't wait to use it to communicate with God. I kept my counselor up very late that night with questions about God, the Trinity, and speaking in tongues.

The camp was to conclude the next morning with a talent show, after which we'd head home in the late afternoon. I hadn't signed up to be in the show, but I couldn't shake this overwhelming desire to express my love and gratitude to God for what He had done. That voice inside—the one I knew and would tell me to use my voice over and over—was encouraging me to use it again. So I went to one of the leaders and asked if I could join the talent show at the last minute. They let me in.

I decided to sing the only church song I knew by heart— "Amazing Grace." After taking the stage, I said to the audience,

"Last night I was filled with the Holy Spirit and spoke in tongues. I feel so much love, and I just want to love Jesus back. I want to sing this song to say thank you to Him for loving me and giving me this gift."

I closed my eyes and began to sing the song from the bottom of my heart. The words never felt more true than they did in that moment. As I sang, I felt an overwhelming sense that this was something I was meant to do my whole life long. My heart swelled with love and adoration as I poured every piece of me into every note of that song.

When I was done, I opened my eyes and looked around. All the leaders were crying, and everyone was applauding. I didn't understand why so many people were crying, but I thought they must just feel the same love that I do.

After the show, person after person came up to me and asked me my name. Nobody knew who I was! The reason everyone kept asking my name became clear later when the time came to announce the camp awards. Apparently this was a decades-old camp tradition. Some awards were silly, like the award for Camp Snoozer, which went to the kid who always missed breakfast because he or she slept in.

After the playful awards and trophies had been handed out, they moved on to the more serious awards: Camp King and Queen. The votes had been counted, and to my complete shock, they called my name. I—the girl nobody knew—was Camp Queen! I had no idea why this was an award or what someone had to do to merit it, but that didn't keep me from drinking in the wonderful way it made me feel. I felt seen, heard, and special. My past and my pain faded away, and I felt the lightheartedness of a girl who is simply a child, without a burden or worry in the world. My only job in that moment was to be happy and enjoy it. As I went up to receive my crown and trophy, the love that had filled me up swirled again inside me, as though I could hear God saying, *I'm so proud of you!*

Amy and I got a ride back home with the pastor of the church that had sent us to the camp. While everyone else fell asleep in the back seat, I sat in the front seat and talked *nonstop* the entire way home. That poor old man—he endured an eleven-year-old girl talking his ear off for three hours straight! I told him I was convinced that I was going to do something great for God. I went on and on about how I could feel it deep down in my bones—God had created me to do something big in this world. Maybe I would be a missionary or a preacher. Whatever it was, I was so excited and overjoyed to feel such a deep sense of purpose and belonging with God. One of the phrases in "Amazing Grace" kept running through my mind: *I once was lost, but now I'm found.* That was exactly what I felt; I felt like I had finally been found.

When to Stop

When we got home, I excitedly told my mom everything that had happened. Then I asked her if we could go to church next Sunday night. I couldn't wait to get back into worship. She agreed, and when Sunday night came, we made our way to church. Right as the worship started, I felt compelled to get out of my seat and go to the front. I lifted my hands and began dancing and singing to Jesus. I didn't know the words to the songs we were singing, so I just sang in tongues. It felt right to do so—to worship God in the language He gave me. It seemed that my own language could not do justice to expressing all the adoration I felt toward God in that moment. I was completely lost in it, without a care in the world. I was worshiping Jesus like I was made to do it all along.

Out of nowhere, I felt two hands grab me and begin pulling me aside. I looked up and saw a woman I didn't know. She was leading me over to a seat. I sat down, stunned and unsure of why she had made me sit down or what was wrong. Moments later, the pastor came to the stage to wrap up the time of worship and transition into the sermon. Most likely, the woman had simply acted because it was time for worship to end, and, being lost in song as I was, I was the only one who didn't know that. But the only reason my little mind and heart could come up with was that I had messed up somehow.

Immediately shame crept into my heart. I felt rejected. My cheeks felt hot and flushed as I put my head down in embarrassment and tried to make sense of it all. I had been lost in worship. It felt so right. It felt like I was doing what I was meant to do. Where did I go wrong? The shame was telling me that my heart wasn't pure and that my motivation in worship wasn't to love Jesus but to draw attention to myself and be a distraction for others.

It was in this moment that the voice that says, *Stop drawing attention to yourself*—which would become terribly familiar— entered my life. I've always had big emotions, and when I want to express something, it usually comes out in a big way. So, naturally, when I got excited about meeting Holy Spirit and catching a taste of God's love for me, I wanted to pour out my love and worship extravagantly. Yet when this voice woke up inside of me, it began a long war between my natural expressiveness and the crushing pressure to shut it all down and withdraw into the shadows. It was the first of countless moments that caused me to question my identity and think that there was something wrong with me and the way I was made.

When we got home that night, I asked my mom why that lady had pulled me away and sat me down. My mom hesitated, like she wasn't sure what to say. Then she said, "Kim, sometimes you have to know when to stop."

I went to my room and sat down to think. I had felt lost in worship—not out of control in a bad or messy way but in a way that was safe and beautiful. But to be told that I need to know when to stop seemed to imply that I was in full control and somehow should have known better. Again, the message I heard was that something was wrong with me—something that had caused me to do something wrong. The shame and embarrassment I felt were overwhelming. Worst of all, I felt rejected by the love that had only a day before felt so life-giving.

And just like that, a silent and giant wall went up around my heart. I felt everything inside me immediately shut down, like a store that had gone out of business and posted signs everywhere: "Closed." I've always been a little dramatic, and this moment was no exception. My heart and all my emotions shut down. I went numb.

The next day, I noticed that when my mom and my sister told me they loved me as usual (before my mom left for work or before we went to bed), I couldn't respond. I felt anger. I didn't want to tell them I loved them. No words came out of me. I just stared blankly and walked away.

As the days passed, the anger built inside me and began to

burst out unexpectedly. I lived on edge, exploding into fits of rage and lashing out at my sister in arguments. The very people I felt so strongly obligated to protect and take care of were the same people on the receiving end of my wrath. I couldn't get control.

After each angry outburst, more shame came rushing in, bringing more rejection, anger, and hopelessness. Rejection told me the church and the people in it hated me. I wasn't good enough, pure enough, or smart enough. Obviously, they knew how to control everything and "when to stop" and I did not.

Anger let me justify myself and step away from the pain. Pain would cause me to look at what had happened and feel the hurt and anger all over again. Anger let me point a finger at that woman who sat me down, like she had it out for me. Anger even let me point a finger at the church camp and all the people in it. *They misled me*, I thought. *This pain is their fault for exposing me to something that for a time made me feel so free but doesn't last.*

My sense of betrayal fueled more rage. I thought Jesus loved me, but He had betrayed me. I thought I mattered and was special. I thought He had a plan for my life. But now, after one embarrassing and confusing experience, I believed it was all a lie. *There is no good future or plan for me*, I concluded. *I was foolish to think that a girl like me could have such a beautiful gift.*

| # BORN AGAIN

When I was twelve, a new man came into my mom's life. His name was George, and he was a strong Christian. After she and George began dating, my mom started taking us to church consistently and making other small changes in our family lifestyle. Church suddenly became very important and didn't seem to be as much of a ritual anymore, but rather something that we began to engage in more seriously.

I still remember the Sunday we got in the car to go to church and she changed the radio station from our normal pop station. Pop music and MTV had always been a constant fixture in our house—Michael Jackson, Whitney Houston, and Huey Lewis and the News were some of my favorites growing up. Dumbstruck, I asked her what on earth we were listening to. She told me it was a Christian radio station and that we were going to start listening to this music. Hunkering down in the back seat, I rolled my eyes, thinking, *I don't like these changes.*

Overall, however, I liked George and thought he was fun. He took us on trips, bought us candy, and taught us what it meant to "stir the pot." This was one of his favorite phrases, and to him it looked like us mischievously teasing our mom while he looked on from around a corner, cracking up. It also looked like the freedom and encouragement to voice our strong opinions. When we asked him if he was going to marry her, he usually responded with a joke and a twinkle in his eye.

But when George followed through on those winks and actually married Mom, everything changed for me. I became convinced that he would be like my other stepfathers and hurt and leave us. He was now a foe against whom I needed to defend and protect my family. On the day of their wedding, I refused to smile for the wedding pictures. I was angry and wanted everyone to know it. When my mom and George returned from their honeymoon, I told George that I did not like him, that I wanted nothing to do with him, and that he was not—and never would be—my dad. I wanted him to know I was done with being hurt by men and would most certainly fight back if he tried anything. I wasn't afraid anymore; I was just plain furious.

"Just Be a Kid"

Much as I had my guard up with George, I had to admit that his marriage to my mom brought a level of comfort, security, and stability to our family that I had never experienced. Right before I started high school, they bought a house, and I got my own bedroom for the first time in my life. I had new clothes to wear and didn't have to worry about going hungry. I was attending the first school where I would stay for longer than two years. All of this was obviously better than the pain, fear, and upheaval we had lived with for so long.

The problem was that I seemed to be the only one who had a problem transitioning from the years of trauma into this new reality, and my relationship with my mom and George grew increasingly strained because of my unresolved anger and pain. There was a months-long period in which we had the same exchange every single Sunday. My mom and George brought me into their bedroom, sat me down, and pleaded with me.

"Why can't you just let go of the past?" Mom would ask. "Why can't you just forget about it?"

She knew my storming around the house yelling, making snotty comments to everyone, and reminding George that he wasn't my dad were not the behaviors of an emotional, hormonal teenager, but were expressions of pain. They had a wounded, broken girl spinning out of control and leaving messes in her wake.

I realize now that they were trying to help me and were probably very tired of dealing with my anger, but their approach didn't work. I wouldn't budge. I tried to explain that it wasn't the same for me as it was for them. My mom had put the past behind her when she married someone new, but I hadn't married someone. I hadn't decided to do something that was a complete detour from where I was. It felt like she had moved on without me and didn't even think about the past anymore, while I was still carrying the wounds and the scars of the past, which were tethering me to the ground somewhere back behind her.

During one of these conversations, my mom seemed to realize that I believed I was responsible to take care of her and protect her. I think she could hear in my language and responses that I carried a sense of responsibility to take care of and protect her and my siblings. It was clear that a lot of my angry actions and outbursts were very defensive. She looked at me with tears in her eyes and said, "Kim, you don't have to take care of me anymore. That is not your job. It's George's job, and he will take care of me and protect me. You're a kid. You just need to be a kid and enjoy that."

She undoubtedly intended for those words to bring freedom and release to me, but they sent me spinning. A world of carefully and strategically placed walls and pillars in my mind came crashing down. I could feel absolute rage bubbling up inside me, creeping up my throat, and practically choking me as it fought to escape. I honestly don't remember if I even responded to her in that moment. The only thing racing through my head was outrage.

Be a kid? BE A KID? I do not have the first clue about what it means to be a kid. I grew up a long time ago. The innocence and the carefree life of a child are so far behind me. I don't know how to be anything other than what I am.

My purpose and identity lay in shambles. If it wasn't my job to take care of and protect my mom and my siblings and I didn't know how to be a kid, then what was I supposed to do? Who was I supposed to be? How was I supposed to behave? What was the point of my life if it was not to take care of and protect my family?

I began a slow, long fall deep down into a very dark pit. The one thought I grabbed on to was that once high school was over, I could escape. If I could just hang in there for these four years, I could leave and start a new life of my own.

I began planning on moving out the moment I graduated. In the meantime, I devoted myself to finding other relationships and pursuits that would give me a sense of meaning. I befriended a ton of people in high school from all social groups—band geeks, athletes, skaters, smart kids, and more. I never wanted anyone to be picked on or left out. As a student, I worked hard and got very involved in all kinds of school activities.

One strange thing that happened early in my freshman year was that I inadvertently made an enemy of my high school choir teacher due to an unfortunate misunderstanding. When he issued a blanket invitation to the choir to participate in a singing competition at a college in a nearby city, I eagerly signed up and paid the fee. Then the teacher informed us he would be selecting our songs for the competition and proceeded to assign me an Italian opera piece. I had no idea how to pronounce any of the words, didn't have a clue as to what I was attempting to sing about, and didn't know anyone who could teach me. So I decided to chuck that song and chose a song that was a big hit that year—Celine Dion's "My Heart Will Go On." We had an option to sing to compete or just to be critiqued, and I had chosen the critique option when I signed up. I only wanted to get some feedback on my singing, so I figured it was best to pick something that would show the judges what I could do.

When the day came, I was standing just outside the stage, waiting to go on, when my teacher appeared and asked if I was ready. I said yes and offhandedly added that I had decided to change my song.

His eyes bugged out as his jaw dropped open in horror. I could practically see the steam coming out of his flaming ears. "Why did you do that?" he practically shouted. With that, he abruptly turned on one foot and stormed offstage. I shrugged my shoulders, wondering why he was so upset. My mom thought it was best that I back out of the event, and I ended up not singing.

The following Monday at school, he kept me after class and chewed me out. "You tried to change years of tradition!" he yelled.

Little did I know that this would go on to be something true of my life in general. My song change decision was apparently offensive enough for him to kick me out of choir and forbid me from ever joining again.

Other than the choir teacher, however, I charmed my other teachers, and they all loved me. I played basketball, ran track, was a cheerleader, joined student council, and poured out a vast amount of passion and excitement in the Thespians Society. And even though I had been banned from choir, I still found a way to keep singing. I performed at pep rallies and sang the national anthem for various sporting events.

I also decided that even though I still didn't know how to resolve the pain of my past, my mom's happiness was extremely important to me. Because of my anger and pain, it was hard for me to go to church. I felt confused. I believed in God and loved God, but I felt angry with Him and struggled to articulate those heavy emotions. But going to church was something very clearly important to my mom, and it made her happy to be involved there. So I wanted to do it. She was on the worship team, and she brought me on to sing with her for various things.

Sometimes I felt flashes of the little girl who met Holy Spirit at a church camp and discovered she loved to worship, but I refused to open my heart to that desire again. I knew how to go through the motions and appear very involved while never fully surrendering to Jesus. My love and care for my mom and for the people at the church were real and genuine, but my relationship with Jesus was not.

Another Crash

My sister and I saw our biological father every other weekend and for a few weeks in the summertime. He often made the long drive down to southern Oregon where we lived to see us or pick us up. Our relationship with him was somewhat fragile. He had never been the same after his motorcycle wreck, and the distance between us made the relationship strained and difficult. But we did love him, and we knew that even when he wasn't good at showing it, he really loved us.

During the summer between my sophomore and junior year, we took a trip to northern Oregon so my sister and I could see our dad, and my mom, George, and my brother could visit my grandparents. When we pulled up to Grandma and Papa's house, they met us outside and pulled my mom aside. I could tell by the look on their faces that something was wrong. My mom walked back over to us and told my sister and me to get back in the car.

My dad had been in another bad motorcycle wreck. It was about a thirty-minute drive to the hospital, and I remember feeling terrified and having so many questions that no one could answer. I cried the whole way as my mom prayed out loud.

When we arrived at the hospital, we were told that he was in the ICU and was somewhat stable but was in a coma and on a breathing machine. We asked if we could see him, and the doctor obliged but warned us that he looked really bad. It was a serious wreck. I followed the doctor down the hallway, and as we drew close to a dimly lit room, I could hear all sorts of machines buzzing, beeping, and pumping. I came around the doorway and there was my dad, surrounded by machines, his body swollen, bruised, and slightly bloody, and his face almost unrecognizable.

I started trembling. I walked slowly toward the bed and reached out a shaking finger to touch his bloody knuckles. Something in the pit of my stomach was churning, trying to erupt out of me. It was a cry—the cry of a little girl, a cry that had been stuffed down for many years. More than fear over the current circumstances, it emerged from years of pain, anguish, and confusion. Unable to hold it in any longer, I let loose with a scream.

"DADDY! DADDY! DADDY!"

The moment these words burst from my mouth, his body started to convulse and move. Alarms and machines started going off, and within seconds, a team of nurses and doctors came running in. They pried my hand from him and pulled me out of the room. I didn't want to stop screaming. I wanted him to wake up. I felt like he was responding to the sound of my voice, just as he had done the first time he was in a coma.

After they ushered me out to the hallway, I was suddenly overwhelmed with dizziness and couldn't see straight. I fell to the floor in a heap of sobs. Someone picked me up and helped me back to the waiting room, my sister and my mom close behind.

We found out later that a car driver had not seen him and turned into him. He was wearing a helmet this time, but unfortunately, it was just not quite enough to limit the damage. The doctor explained that there was a lot of scar tissue and deterioration in his brain from the first accident and that his chances of survival and coming out of the coma were very low. People rarely survived two head injuries with that kind of severity. If he did wake up, the doctor thought there was little likelihood of him functioning normally.

My sister and I visited him every day. We talked and sang to him. During each visit, I asked him to squeeze my hand if he could hear me, and I swore he did every time, though the other adults in the room looked at me with pitying smiles of disbelief.

To the shock and amazement of all the doctors, one day my

dad woke up. Not only did he wake up, but he slowly began to regain his faculties and functions. Like the first time, it required a very long, difficult journey with countless hospital visits and rehab, but he again regained the ability to walk and talk. It was tough for us as teens to fully understand everything we saw during the healing process. Once again, he was not quite the same person. As his brain was trying to heal, he said funny things, claimed he remembered things that didn't actually happen, and had wild fits of rage and unresponsiveness. Those were very scary moments. But little by little, he continued to improve and function somewhat normally again.

Fear versus Faith

Then, while my dad was still rehabilitating, another blow fell. I walked through the door after school one day and instantly knew something was wrong. There were about four other people at our house, all of them sitting in the living room, and I could see that everyone was teary-eyed but kind of trying to hide it. My mom was sitting on the couch close to George, holding his hand.

"Kim, I need to talk to you," my mom said. "Can we go to your room?"

"Okay," I said. My voice sounded soft and squeaky, like I had forgotten how to talk.

We walked to my room and sat down on my bed. My mom took a breath and said, "I have breast cancer. I'm going to have a big surgery, and I'll need to have chemotherapy after that. But I'm going to fight this, and I know that God will heal me," she said, squeezing my hand.

I could barely hear anything she said after her first sentence: "I have breast cancer." I was stunned. *Was my mom going to die? How long do we have? What is chemotherapy?* My mind was running wild, and I was so scared and in shock. I didn't know what to do or say, and nothing made sense.

I wanted to be the only kind of Kim I knew how to be—the Kim who takes care of her mom. I wanted to find a way to fix this or at least make it better. But as this situation unfolded, it was abundantly clear, again and again, that it was completely out of my control. I watched as my mom underwent a huge surgery that left her with scars and tubes hanging out of her body. I helped her change out the tubes, cleaned her wounds, and hugged her while she cried as she looked at herself in the mirror. I watched as all her hair fell out during chemotherapy, which made her terribly sick. There were times she'd lie in bed, too weary and sick to move. A few of those times, I opened her door to check on her and was struck with terror at the sight of her lying there, motionless. It took all my courage to walk over to the bed and reach out a shaking hand to see if she was still breathing.

George showed incredible strength and love for my mom during this ordeal. He was attentive to her, carrying her, encouraging her, making her laugh, and helping her in any way he could. He stayed positive and confident and spoke with a lot of faith whenever we discussed how Mom was doing. But I also saw him in tender moments when he prayed for her or cried with her.

Both George and my mom seemed to have a level of confidence that their prayers would be answered and that she would survive this ordeal, but I struggled to share this feeling with them. I remember one week when George was away on a business trip, my brother, who was only seven at the time, had the flu.

My mom couldn't take care of him, not only because of how sick she was, but because she couldn't afford to be exposed to a virus with an immune system compromised from the chemotherapy.

I stayed home from school to take care of my brother and my mom. I remember part of me feeling glad to have the chance to do what I had always done and take care of everyone, while another part of me was terrified and worried every day about whether my mom would survive, and yet another part was angry, tired, and completely ticked off at this God who had seemingly abandoned me as a child and just wouldn't let up with the suffering. It was like we couldn't catch a break. *Where is He?*—the question of my freaking life.

From the moment Mom told us her diagnosis, she had repeatedly stated that she believed God would heal her and she would be okay. She showed incredible strength as she continued to work through the whole ordeal and attend school functions. At the time, I couldn't tell if she really believed that or if she was just trying to appear strong and full of faith for us, her kids. But one day, some people from our church came to our house to pray for my mom and anoint her with oil. She also had us, her children, pray for her. Afterward, she told us that during that prayer time, she'd had a moment of breakthrough where she felt like God healed her. At the time, I only thought, *I'll believe it when I see it.*

Yet as the days and weeks unfolded, she proceeded to recover, defying all the odds and astounding the doctors. Her strength returned more and more every day, and she began to look and sound more like herself. She had periodic blood tests to see if she still had cancer inside her, and every time she got her results back, there was no sign of cancer. The doctor told her that the cancer was in "remission" and would most likely show back up, but my mom absolutely refused to believe that. Test after test came back cancer-free.

My mom had her last surgery when I was in my first year of college. She came down to California to visit me, and I threw her a "Happy No More Surgeries" party. I decorated her hotel room, bought her gifts, and even made two cakes that were shaped and frosted to look like breasts! To this day she has been cancer-free, proving all the doctor's predictions false and confirming that God had indeed healed her.

A Long Slide Down a Dark Hole

Enduring these life-threatening crises in my parents' lives intensified the primary areas of pain, fear, and confusion in my life. On the one hand, I was, in a way, strangely comfortable in the face of trauma, because that was what I had lived through-out my life. It was refreshing and familiar to have moments and opportunities to step back into my old role of taking care of my family members. Yet on the other hand, the fact remained that I was reliving the horror that had turned my world upside down as a child—nearly losing my father, watching his tortured recovery, and then facing the possibility of losing my mother as well.

At the center of this was my wrestling match with God. He was the only one we could turn to in these terrifying circumstances, yet He was also the one who had let these things happen throughout my life. So even when both of my parents survived and the stories had a good ending, this did little to bring healing to my heart. Instead, my pain, my struggle with my identity, and my sense of loneliness and being abandoned by God intensified.

It was in this season that I began to live a double life. At home, I stayed busy taking care of everyone and trying to keep them in good spirits. At school and in the community, I was the happy girl who participated in everything and was an over-achiever; I competed in pageants and won, gaining recognition in our small town. Many parents knew me as the reliable babysitter they could count on to take care of and love their children. And I continued to attend and be active at church with my family.

At the same time, I was locking my bedroom door at night, cranking up the volume on my TV or CD player, and climbing out of my window to sneak out with friends. I dated boys and tried to feel some sense of love and significance. I secretly went to parties and drank, trying to numb my pain. Somehow my mom usually found out about these parties and asked me if I had been there, but every time I lied and denied it.

When I was alone in my room, the same lies that had taunted me throughout my life returned, only now they were louder and more convincing than ever: *You are alone. Your life is not worth living. You should end it.* These made sense to me. These were the messages that seemed to echo through everything that had happened to me since I was a child. I heard them in my loneliness as a little girl crying in bed at night, wishing her parents had never divorced. I felt them in the way my former stepdads had made me feel worthless. They spoke in my shame when I had apparently selfishly wanted attention as a little girl dancing and worshiping at church.

I couldn't see any value for myself or a place for me in this world. I didn't know how to be a kid. I had been robbed of my childhood and told it was no longer my job to take care of my family. Despite all the roles I was playing at school, church, and in the community, I had zero sense of identity. The thought of trying to grow up was absolutely terrifying, because I thought I would just relive what I had already gone through, except as an adult. I couldn't see any hope of a different outcome in my life.

Eventually the lies, hopelessness, pain, and rage began to reach unbearable levels of torment inside me, and death increasingly seemed like the only way out.

One day at church, I was sitting alone during the ministry time while everyone around me was praying or wrapped up in a moment with Jesus. A friend of my mom came over to me, gave me a big hug, and asked if she could pray for me. I agreed, and she began to pray. Then suddenly she stopped, looked up at me with tears in her eyes, grabbed my face, and asked, "Have you been thinking about suicide?"

I immediately turned red, fought to hold in my tears, and slightly nodded my head. The woman practically started shouting in tongues. She too was a mama, and I knew she loved me. In that moment, she was praying for me, fighting for me, and strongly coming against the lies I was believing. She urged me not to listen to the voice of the enemy speaking lies over me. She told me how special I was and how much I mattered. But for a girl living with years of lies and pain, it was very hard to believe.

A few months after this encounter, early in my senior year, I was home alone and feeling overwhelmed by it all. I literally could not take another moment of my life, and I saw no way out but one. I went to the medicine cabinet and began grabbing a bunch of different pills. I didn't know what every item was—everything from Tylenol to my mom's cancer drugs was in there.

When I had a huge handful, I swallowed them and burst into tears, sobbing in desperation. Eventually I blacked out.

Some time later, I woke up. I was surprised to see that I was still in my house and lying on the floor. I glanced at the clock. Only two hours had passed. I looked around me and saw no vomit or any sign that I had been sick. I felt nothing in my body—not a stomachache, a headache, nothing. Then a thought suddenly floated into my mind.

There must be a God, and He must really love me.

I didn't know why—I couldn't fathom why—but I knew He had saved me from death. Not because I had done anything to earn being saved. I could only imagine grace that we do not always understand. And in that moment, I felt His love burst through my pain. I hadn't felt His love so powerfully since I was eleven years old at church camp, but in that encounter, His love had been an awakening. This time it was like a wrecking ball.

I could hear Him shouting His love over me. In a moment, the lies of shame and worthlessness that had bound me like heavy chains seemed to fall away. I felt light as a feather. I knew I was loved. I knew my life had value to Him. I knew I was here for a purpose. I knew I was wanted. These waves of truth flooded my parched soul, and I drank them in like my life depended on it. My shoulders were heaving as I wailed and shouted to Him, "I surrender!"*

Right there on the floor, I committed my life to Him. Now

---

* In narrating this experience, I am simply conveying the thoughts and feelings that occurred to me as truthfully as I know how. These in no way are meant to suggest that those lost through suicide are any less loved, wanted, or worth saving by God. If you or someone you know is struggling with depression, torment, or suicidal thoughts, I encourage you to reach out to the National Suicide Prevention Lifeline at 1-800-273-TALK (8255).

that I saw the lies for what they were, I felt stirred by a righteous anger to fight for my life and my heart. From that moment on, I was moving forward into a new life of freedom with Jesus—no going back. I had no clear memory as a child asking Jesus into my heart—this was definitely the moment I fully committed my heart to Him and vowed to spend my life pursuing Him.

Every senior at my high school was required to complete a big project, and I chose to record an album. I chose this project because of how much I loved singing and because I wanted others to hear how much Jesus loves them and come to know the freedom that Christ offered them. I sat in my bedroom alone for hours, writing and rewriting lyrics that attempted to communicate what God had done in me. I used an old recorder that had belonged to my mom to record the melodies I composed for the lyrics.

I didn't play an instrument, but I had a producer who listened to the recording and built the music around them. As was the case with most professional songwriters, I don't think my early songs were very good, but they were so genuine and pure in their expression. I just wanted to create something that expressed my love for Jesus and what He had done for me, and these songs did that with a high level of vulnerability—something that is still characteristic of my writing and singing today. Just as I had done all those years ago at church camp, my response to encountering Jesus was to pour out worship and adoration toward Him. It was the beginning of the pattern that would unfold throughout my life.

I wrote my heart out and spent the year recording the album. When it was finished, I was so proud of this gift I was giving back to Jesus. My favorite of all my songs I wrote at that time was called "Freedom":

Born Again

I've been struggling with my past.
It just clings to me and holds me back.
It grips my heart and it won't let go.
I can't find or face my tomorrow
Full of anger, guilt, and rage.
How do I let go of every page?
I can't move on, and I won't go back.
Where do I go to stop this attack?
Now here I stand in a different place.
Will I choose to let go and win the race?
Lord, You call me forward and say, "Look to Me."
Slowly I find myself drop to my knees.
Father, You hold me so close.
I surrender my past, and You sweep it away.
I won't turn around, and there's no looking back.
I give my life away and find Your freedom.
It feels so good to let go,
So good to be sure and to know
That Your freedom has come and Your freedom will stay.
For who You set free is free for always.

Chapter 5 NEW EYES

Not long after giving my life to Jesus, I decided I wanted to attend a Christian college. I applied to Oral Roberts University in Tulsa, Oklahoma, and I soon learned that I had been accepted and awarded a music scholarship.

Then one day while praying in my backyard, I heard the still, small voice of God telling me to go to Redding, California. It wasn't an audible command. It was just the words "Redding, California" popping into my mind and a sense that I needed to obey. I wasn't sure where Redding was or if there was a school there, but an online search led me to a Christian college called Simpson University. I quickly applied, doubting I would get in since it was so close to the deadline, but they accepted me.

When I announced to my family the change of plans, they were less than thrilled that I was giving up a scholarship and heading in a completely different direction. But I knew in my heart it was the right decision.

My confidence was soon tested, however, as my freshman year at Simpson unfolded. My plan to major in music faltered after only a few days of trying to learn to sight-read in my first semester ear-training class. After switching my major to history, I continued to struggle academically despite my best efforts, earning a 1.2 GPA in my first semester. I decided my teachers just didn't know how to teach a creative genius like myself who didn't hesitate to push back when I disagreed with their methods. For example, I once challenged the teacher of my writing and literature class on why she had graded me so poorly, arguing that she clearly had marked me down because she didn't agree with my point of view.

My willingness to debate with both teachers and students did not win me many likability points. On another memorable occasion in the school cafeteria, I got into an argument with a guy I didn't know about whether women could be anything more than a wife and mother according to God's Word. It was obvious he was better versed in Scripture than I was, but I couldn't resist pushing back against his repugnant ego.

He argued that the only place for women, according to Scripture, was the home. While a husband and family were things I earnestly desired, it was certainly not the only aspiration of my heart. And I felt sure that Jesus had placed these other desires in my heart, just as He has for many women. In my newness to Scripture, I couldn't come up with anything to contest him, but I made sure he knew that if he was looking for a wife, he was certainly looking in the wrong place.

Hoping to make some friends, I decided to audition for the chapel worship team as a background singer. At the audition, they put the whole group of potential background singers onstage and had us sing together for what seemed like only fifteen seconds. I didn't make the team—not too surprising, given the fact that the audition didn't really give us the chance to show anything (or maybe they secretly required sight-singing skills and knew I didn't have any). But it did add to my discouragement and confusion. I couldn't understand why the Lord had brought me to Simpson.

The Church on the Hill

One night a group of students invited me to a worship gathering called Celebration that was led by a guy named Nathan Edwardson. A local church had given him permission to host these nights of worship. I found myself in a dimly lit room full of young adults worshiping and singing. I didn't recognize the songs, but I did notice that the band was quite good. Between songs the worship leaders talked about things like worshiping in "the secret place" and being "a nameless, faceless generation"—phrases I hadn't heard before, but which stirred something deep in my heart. The whole evening I just sat in the back and cried, unable to put language to what I was feeling and experiencing.

I continued to attend Celebration, and each time I experienced something new in worship. One evening the entire band led worship from behind a curtain. The leader, Nathan, explained that it was important for us to have our own connection to the Lord and to worship Him in our own way. The worship wasn't about the band leading or the songs they were singing, but simply about Jesus. Again I was moved and drawn to what I was hearing and experiencing. What was so different about these people and their connection with God? What exactly was I lacking?

Sometime toward the end of first semester, the pressure cooker of emotions that had been building through my frustration with Simpson and this strange spiritual hunger in worship finally exploded late one night after I left a Celebration gathering. As I drove through Redding on my way back to campus, I broke down crying and screaming out to God in the darkness. "Why am I here? I'm lonely. My grades are horrible. I don't like school! Why did You bring me here?"

In my overwrought state, I made a wrong turn getting back to campus and found myself driving down a road that dead-ended at a building perched on one side of a hill. It was a circular building with a steeple that glowed a soft red. Through wrap-around windows, I glimpsed a few people inside, and out of curiosity I parked my car to watch. I saw one woman dancing off to one side, while another woman stood facing the window with hands lifted, crying, her lips moving as if she was praying or singing. Two men were pacing across the room, waving what appeared to be scarves and, I assumed, praying.

What a bunch of weirdos! I thought.

I drove a little closer to investigate the larger building and saw that it was a church. The name on the sign read "Bethel Church." Intrigued, I decided I would check it out that coming weekend.

On Sunday morning, I walked into the main sanctuary and found it full of excited, happy people. As worship started, I was surprised to see individuals around the room waving flags, dancers on the stage, and a huge band with more instruments than I had ever seen in church. Everyone around me was singing and worshiping with passion, and I soon felt the same hunger I had felt at Celebration stirring inside me.

At the same time, however, I experienced a powerful surge of fear. Was it fear of the unknown? Fear of rejection? Whatever it was, it was unbearable, and I jumped up and ran out of the room. Tears stung my eyes as I drove away from the church, struggling to understand the turmoil inside me. Overwhelmed, I decided to stuff my feelings down, lock them up, and tell myself that those people were all just too weird and happy for me.

I continued to visit different churches each Sunday, trying to find a place that felt right. I also kept going to Celebration, searching for answers to the questions inside me. But as the weeks passed, I couldn't stop thinking about Bethel Church. Finally I decided to give it another try.

This time an usher greeted me at the door. Upon hearing that I was a student at Simpson, he said, "You should meet Angelina," and he led me over to a girl I recognized as a member of the dance team. It turned out that Angelina and I lived only a couple of dorms apart on campus. Within weeks we became fast friends—a friendship that immediately made my life in Redding a hundred times more bearable. Though I continued to struggle in school, I no longer felt so alone. She also answered my questions about Bethel, and when she didn't know an answer, she helped me look for it in the Bible. Eventually she invited me to help out with the youth group on Wednesdays, assuring me that they always needed more help and that I would be welcome. She introduced me to the youth pastor, Banning Liebscher. It felt good to find a place not only to belong but to be of service. I loved it so much that I stuck around.

When my year at Simpson ended, I returned home to Oregon for the summer and started praying about what I should do next. There was an internship program in Seattle, Washington, connected with my parents' church that my family really wanted me to attend. But I knew I needed to figure out why God had sent me to Redding and what my time there had been about.

In the end, I decided to go with my gut and return to Redding—this time to attend the ministry school at Bethel. My mom was in tears, full of worry. She didn't know much about the church or the school, and she was nervous about what I was going to do with my life. I didn't want to admit it, but I was nervous too! What *was* I going to do with my life? I had no idea. All I knew was that something was pulling me strongly in this direction, and I was desperate to discover what might satisfy the hunger inside me.

In the Silence

Within the first couple of weeks of ministry school, an announcement came that worship team auditions would be taking place. Just as I was about to sign up, however, I felt a conviction and heard the Lord's familiar voice speaking gently to me: "I don't want you to sing. I don't want you to tell anyone you sing. I will bring this back in My time. Right now, in this season, I want you to learn to hear My voice." It wasn't an audible voice. It was a comforting voice inside me that is as familiar as the wind on my skin or the sun shining in my eyes.

Obediently, I didn't sign up for the auditions. At first this decision felt fine to me, but within days, I realized that God's words had set me on a journey. All the questions inside me, the things I couldn't seem to put words to, were about to come to the surface and find some answers.

Worship was part of each day at ministry school. Again and again during these first months, I opened my mouth to sing along with my classmates, and nothing would come out. It was as though I had lost my voice or forgotten how to sing. Then I would hear the still small voice say, "Listen," and I would fall to the floor in class in a pile of sobs. I was so overcome with emotion that I couldn't even stop to consider what my peers were thinking. Were they staring at me? Did they think I was crazy? I didn't even care. I knew that God was doing something profound in my heart.

I couldn't have predicted I would feel this way, but having my singing voice taken away made me feel like I was standing empty-handed with nothing to call my own. Singing was something I had done my whole life, and despite the debacle with my high school choir teacher, it was the one thing I knew I could do well. My whole family was musical, and I had been put on a stage since I was three years old. I had always been involved in musicals, and singing was just something that felt natural and easy. I wasn't a great athlete. I didn't make good grades. After seeing me try to thicken spaghetti sauce with breadcrumbs, my mom begged me to stay out of the kitchen. I wasn't particularly crafty or artistic. But I could sing. What was more, I saw it as the main way to express myself before God. And in asking me not to sing but to listen, God was exposing the truth that much of my identity was wrapped up in this one thing. I realized that I had no idea who I was or what I was created for.

Yet there in the confusion and emptiness, I also recognized the tender love of Jesus. Very gently and with so much kindness, He was beginning to show me who I am. He wanted me to see that I am simply His daughter and that He wanted everything in my life to be anchored to that truth. Each day it felt as though more of the pain and lies I had believed my whole life were fading away and Jesus was there, assuring me of His love for me and the fact that I belong to Him. Yet as amazing as this was, I sensed that we were only just beginning the heart odyssey on which He was leading me.

Healing Begins

I made a friend at the school of ministry named Jodi. She helped me understand many of the things Jesus was teaching me in that season, and I found it easy to trust and confide in her. Jodi was training with a counselor at the church and knew a lot about inner healing. She was also very discerning and quickly saw what I didn't fully see for myself—that I was very wounded and carrying a lot of pain from my past. The effects of my childhood showed up in my triggered responses to things like stress, new environments, and confrontation. But like so many people who grow up with abuse, trauma, and dysfunction, I didn't really recognize how much baggage I was carrying around, because I didn't know any better. While I suspected that some of my reactions to things weren't quite right, I thought, *Isn't this how life is for everybody?*

It wasn't until Jodi gently explained that my behavior bore clear signs of childhood trauma and encouraged me to see a counselor that I began to understand I was pretty messed up inside. She recommended I meet with Teresa, a counselor with whom she had been training, and offered to accompany me to a session. I can't say I fully understood what inner healing was, but I was curious and knew well enough that I needed help to be set free from my past, so I agreed to a trial session.

When we feel sick and not quite right, we go to a doctor. We surrender to the doctor's examination, diagnosis, and prescribed treatment. We may not know what's wrong, but we can recognize that we need some help. I didn't know what was broken inside me, but I knew I needed Jesus. If there was anyone who could step into the dark, pain-filled rooms of my heart, shine light on the broken places, and bring healing and freedom, it was Him.

Teresa began our session by praying and inviting Jesus to fill the room, lead us, and do whatever He wanted to do. She asked me simple questions: "Can you sense or see Jesus? How do you feel about Him?" And then she asked me a strange question: "Would anybody else like to speak?"

What kind of crazy question is that? I thought. *What does it even mean?* But to my surprise, I answered her. In fact, I shouted.

"I am so angry at Jesus!"

The voice was my own, and at the same time it wasn't me. It felt as though I was outside of my body for a moment and someone else was responding. I didn't say much after that.

When the session ended, I felt bewildered and a little embarrassed. However, Teresa assured me I was definitely okay and not losing my mind. She said that when children go through traumatic experiences, it is normal for their brain to dissociate and create another "person" to handle the pain and trauma. It's a coping mechanism that can be important for the child to use in order to survive whatever trauma they are facing. She referred to these other parts of me as "fractures" and said that Jesus wanted to bring total healing to my heart, soul, and personality by integrating these fractured pieces into a whole.

Wholeness sounded pretty good.

All of this made sense, and I could feel the truth of it deep inside me. I sat quietly as I considered everything Teresa was saying. I suddenly remembered an early memory of when I was a little girl about five years old. I woke up one night to the sound of my sister crying, and I realized we weren't in our beds. We were somewhere else—in fact, we were in a different house. I was so scared, but something in me was determined that I needed to be brave in that moment and take care of my sister.

I wrapped my arms around her and tried my best to soothe and assure her. In that moment, I felt like someone else inside me stepped up to protect us, while the Kim who was scared and wanted to cry, just like my sister was doing, went into hiding. I comforted her by putting my arm around her and telling her that everything was going to be okay. I told her I would find our mom and make sure nothing happened to her. This was the first memory where I recognized the fracturing Teresa was referring to.

I continued to meet regularly with Teresa to pursue this integration process of healing. As the months progressed, I had some very good days and some very hard days. I became more aware of these other fractured pieces of myself and began to visualize them in my mind like a room full of people. Teresa helped me use this visualization to allow the fractures to speak to her and to Jesus.

For example, one day I visualized one of these fractures talking to Teresa and explaining that she was young and very scared and really just wanted someone to take care of her. Teresa introduced her to Jesus and asked her if she would like to go to Him as He stood there with outstretched arms. She wasn't sure she could trust Him and felt like she needed to consult the other parts. She wanted an assurance from Jesus that He would take care of her and protect her.

At one point, while Jesus was assuring her He would take good care of her, He told her that she was a smart girl. For whatever reason, this was a very important statement to this part of me. I was believing the lie that I am not smart. The moment

Jesus said that, I began to cry. As the power of this lie was broken, I watched as that fractured part of me walked to Jesus, embraced Him, and disappeared into Him.

It was a good day whenever one of these "parts" went running into the arms of Jesus and disappeared—becoming integrated—as He brought healing. I once asked Teresa why parts would disappear when they went to Jesus and I became integrated in that moment.

She asked me, "Does Jesus live inside you?"

"Yes," I responded.

"Because Jesus lives inside you, when they disappear inside Him, they are also disappearing inside you," she explained. "This is the integration. The pieces of your heart are being put back together. Christ is in you, and you are in Christ."

However, I also had bad days when I refused to talk and didn't want any healing. Fear and anger were always on the surface on those days. One day Teresa and I started our time together, as we always did, by inviting Jesus to come and do what He wanted to do. The moment I visualized Jesus coming into the room, it was as if that fractured group inside my mind began to throw rocks at Him in anger. I sat there silently, feeling rage surge inside me but not daring to speak about what I was seeing in my mind.

Suddenly my thoughts were interrupted by Teresa's voice. "You can't throw rocks at Jesus," she said with a smile. "You can throw something soft, like fruit, but not rocks."

I froze, stunned. She could see what I was seeing in my mind. I felt exposed, yet at the same time, I felt the compassion of Jesus. In His mercy and kindness, He had set me in a safe place with a trustworthy person who could lead me toward total healing and restoration. In this moment, God had allowed her to see what I was seeing in my mind so that she could teach me something I really needed to understand.

Teresa understood that Jesus is not afraid of my anger, nor is He repelled by it. As a person with very big emotions, it felt so good to realize that it's okay for me to experience big and sometimes negative emotions. It's not okay for me to act out in demeaning or hurtful ways because of them. Her simple statement enabled me to let go of some control and surrender my anger a little more. The raging parts in me put down their rocks, and something like reverence toward Jesus emerged, along with greater trust that He could heal me.

Asking the Questions

One weekend a couple of months into my healing journey, I went home to visit my family in Oregon. It was a difficult time. I didn't feel ready to talk to my family members about the healing I was fighting for, and I felt raw and vulnerable. Talking about things that happened in the past was not something we did in my family. In many ways, I already felt like a different, freer person, yet I didn't know how to introduce them to that person when they knew me as someone else.

After enduring a few uncomfortable days, I decided to drive back to Redding a little earlier than usual on Sunday so I could attend the evening service at Bethel. I walked into church a few minutes late and made my way toward the front. Immediately tears began to flow—tears of relief to be in worship, as well as tears of frustration with my current state of brokenness.

There was a guest worship leader that night named Anthony Skinner. As he began to sing, I closed my eyes and immediately saw Jesus standing in front of me with His arms outstretched in welcome. Call it a vision, a dream, or something random in my mind—He was so real in that moment. I started sobbing as I realized that I wanted so badly to be in His arms and close to Him, yet also I was aware that I didn't deserve to be there. I felt ashamed and so broken that I couldn't even look at His face. Then Jesus moved toward me, and I couldn't resist or put up a fight anymore. I collapsed in His arms and turned my face away, weeping. Fear of rejection and shame coursed through me, causing me to shrink to the floor.

Suddenly two questions floated into my mind:

How much do You love me?

What were You thinking when You created me?

Though I later recognized that this was the Holy Spirit exposing the deepest questions of my heart to lead me into more healing, in that moment, there was no way on God's green earth that I was going to ask those questions. I thought I already knew the answers.

For many years, that idea I had picked up as a young girl— that my dad's disappointment in not having a boy meant that I was somehow a mistake—had led me to believe that God had messed up when He created me. So I thought asking God what He was thinking when He created me would just be asking Him to explain what a mistake I was. I expected Him to say, "Well, I was trying to make a boy, but whoops! You came out a girl." I had always believed I should have been a boy. And to ask Him, "How much do You love me?" Well, how much could you possibly love such a mistake? I couldn't risk hearing the rejection I thought would inevitably come.

I hunkered down, refusing to respond to Holy Spirit's invitation. Suddenly I heard Anthony Skinner speaking into the microphone.

"You need to ask Jesus two questions," he said.

My heart started pounding. *This cannot be happening.*

"You need to ask Jesus, 'How much do You love me?'" he said. "And 'What were You thinking when You created me?'"

I was completely shocked and furious. This visiting worship leader had just called me out and exposed me in front of everyone! Of course Anthony did not single me out in any way—he was undoubtedly just communicating what he felt the Holy Spirit was saying. But I felt like he had just listened to my private conversation and then blasted the details over a megaphone for the entire room to hear.

I closed my eyes and returned my thoughts and attention to this moment I was having with Jesus in my mind and heart. Realizing I was not getting away from this, I mustered up all the courage I could, turned my face toward Jesus, and asked, "How much do You love me?"

Immediately I saw Jesus throw His arms open wide and say, "I love you this much!" His arms began to stretch as far as my eyes could see and beyond. He was laughing with so much joy. It was as if He had been waiting a long time to answer this question in me. I looked to the left and the right and couldn't see an end to how far His arms were stretching. Realizing there was no end to His love for me, I began sobbing and laughing with joy. I was so amazed that He expressed His love toward me in a way that felt so fitting for who I am and the way I think.

It was very childlike and joyful. *He speaks my language,* I thought. I was overwhelmed at a love that would call out to me directly, in the midst of a worship set with hundreds of people, just to pull me in to a moment of healing. To feel the love of God felt like sunshine breaking through an eternity of winter. The cold and bleakness of loneliness was suddenly replaced with the warmth of being seen and known. I felt so content and at peace that I thought, *There's no need to ask the second question.* Or so I assumed.

Weeks later I was spending an early morning at Bethel's prayer chapel—that's what the circular building with the red steeple turned out to be—reading my Bible and praying. All of a sudden, I felt the presence of God in the room so strongly. The entire atmosphere seemed to change. The hairs on the back of my neck stood up, and a tingly, excited anticipation flooded my heart. Jesus felt so close. Instantly I knew what He had come for. He wanted me to ask my second question. I couldn't believe it. I was hoping He had forgotten! My heart was pounding, and I could feel tears sting my eyes. It was as if Jesus was tapping me on my shoulder from behind and saying, "Kim, please ask Me."

Maybe if I start singing and worshiping, He'll forget about it, I thought. *Maybe if I read my Bible a little more, He'll stop asking.* But the tug on my heart didn't stop. Just as before, I gave in and fell to the floor as huge, choking sobs burst from me. I could barely get the words out as I asked Jesus, "What were You thinking when You created me?"

I was stretched out on the floor, face down against the carpet, and my eyes were burning from the tears pouring out of them. As I closed my eyes, and just as soon as the question left my mouth, a picture appeared in my mind. I was standing beside Jesus, and we were both facing God the Father across a table. The Father suddenly reached into His chest, grabbed His heart, and ripped off a chunk of it. He threw it down on the table, and it became clay. As He began shaping and molding it, I realized it was me. When He was finished, He reached over, grabbed a box, and placed me inside it. Confused, I turned to Jesus and asked what was going on. Jesus responded, "Shh. Watch."

The Father stood in front of the box with a look of excitement and anticipation on His face. Suddenly He threw open the box, and the little me began dancing, singing, and worshiping Him. It was like a girl's jewelry box with a tiny ballerina inside that twirls to music when you open it. The Father became so excited and shouted, "Woohoo!" as He jumped and twirled around. Then He shut the box, waited with great anticipation, and threw the lid open again. Once more I sang and danced, and He ran around shouting for joy. I stood there watching Him repeat the same sequence of events over and over. I was bewildered at His excitement for me.

Then the Father reached into the box and put me in the palm of His hand. In that moment, my perspective changed—I went from watching all of this along the side to being there in His hand. He was pulling me close to His heart, and as I got closer, I could see the outline of the place where He had ripped out the piece to make me. He slid me into that spot, and I fit perfectly, like a puzzle piece. As I nestled into His heart, I could feel the warmth of His love.

Then I heard the Father begin to speak. "You are not a mistake. I knew exactly what I was doing when I created you. I am so happy you are a girl! I made you simply because you make me so happy. You bring me so much joy! I love it when you worship me and sing to me. I love every single thing about you. You make me laugh! I think you are funny. This is the place you were made from and this is where you stay, here in my heart, so close to me. Nobody else can fill this spot. It's just for you."

I could hardly breathe from the weeping that wracked me throughout this encounter. Years of pain and toxic beliefs slipped away as His love surrounded and filled me. As God spoke out His love for me, it was as if the vibrations from His voice were a wave of love rolling over the walls around my heart, causing them to begin to crumble. My heart felt like it was beginning to truly beat and come alive for the first time.

When You Invite Jesus into the Room

These encounters with God's love brought a new level of hope and joy to my heart. However, I could still feel there were broken pieces of me that I had not yet surrendered to healing. I felt as though I had gotten to a certain degree of closeness with Him, but there was a thin veil separating us and keeping me from getting closer. I could see Him on the other side, and I wanted to be there too, but I kept holding back part of my heart. I began to realize I didn't fully trust Him yet—it was as if I was saying to Jesus that He could have a lot of my heart, but not all of it. Even after feeling and encountering His amazing love, I still felt deep inside me that He could not be trusted with all of me.

Questions lingered. *Why did all the bad things happen? Why was I abused? Why was I not protected? Why did You let me live in so much fear? You are God. You could have stopped those things at any moment, but You didn't. Where were You?* These questions bounced around in my mind with increasing intensity and soon became tormenting. I could see they were holding me back from the total freedom for which I longed, but I couldn't seem to let them go. They loomed like a mountain inside me, and no matter how hard I prayed or analyzed or tried to push it away, I just couldn't make it move.

Finally one day I hit my breaking point. I couldn't take it any longer. I wanted to be free so badly. I wanted to experience the fullness of Jesus' presence with nothing between us. And so I made a decision. I decided that my desire for Him was greater than my need for explanations. I was willing to surrender my questions if it meant I could finally lift the veil that seemed to shroud my spirit. Aloud, I made this declaration: "Jesus, I want You more than I want the answers."

That night I had a bizarre dream. I saw a strange object, and after staring at it for a while, I realized I was looking at a chunk of flesh. Something was moving underneath its surface, as though trying to break through. Suddenly it did, and I saw an eye. It squinted in the light, retracted into the flesh, and then popped back up again.

When I woke up the next morning and remembered the dream, I thought, *That was crazy. What did I eat last night?*

Just then I heard the Lord's still small voice say, "You are getting new eyes today."

As those words echoed through my mind, I felt a trembling inside me. Something was about to break. Something was about to change.

I went to work that morning and headed to ministry school in the afternoon. By the time I arrived at the church, the inner trembling had increased so much that it was all I could do to hold myself together.

Seeing the state I was in, one of my teachers, who knew

about the healing process I had been walking through, called Teresa and told her she should come right away to pray for me. Within minutes, Teresa and Jodi showed up with two other women, and we all headed to a private room. I could feel a huge *something* about to bubble to the surface inside me. We sat down, and Teresa immediately prayed and invited Jesus to come.

I closed my eyes, and in my mind, I saw all of us sitting in that little office together. Then I saw Jesus enter this picture and walk into the room with us. Immediately I couldn't hold it in any longer. I began to scream.

"I hate You!"

Everything I had felt for so long but never wanted to say began pouring out of me, my whole body trembling as I sobbed and wailed. Every fractured piece of me was howling at Jesus in furious rage and unspeakable pain.

"Where were You? I was a child! You weren't there. I hate You!"

I saw Jesus walking toward me, completely unfazed.

"You abandoned me!" I continued, shaking with anger. "You let me down. You didn't protect me."

Then Jesus reached me. Slowly and gently He wrapped His arms around me and drew me in close, silently holding me as I screamed and shouted.

At last, when my strength failed and my angry words were spent, I began to weep. I cried and cried for what felt like hours. It was as though a dam had broken and years of stored-up tears were gushing out in that moment. And one by one, each fractured part of me walked into Jesus until there was only one me left. Total integration.

Gradually I began to grow calm, and new tears began to flow—tears that came from the revelation that I was not rejected.

I had unleashed all my fury at Jesus, and He had not responded with anger. He didn't punish me or walk away from me. He didn't yell at me, condemn me, or tell me what a bad Christian I was. He only loved me. He didn't demand perfection. He didn't expect me to clean everything up and present something shiny and pure. He met me right where I was. Oh, what overwhelming, amazing love!

As I opened my eyes, I was stunned. Everything around me was vibrant with color and life. Teresa, Jodi, and everybody else in the room looked different. Colors looked different. There was so much light. It was as if I had been living in a world of gray and heaviness, viewing all of life through a clouded lens of pain, and now that lens had been removed. I truly did get new eyes that day.

This experience was one of my greatest moments of breakthrough. At last I felt like I could really breathe. I felt completely free!

Looking Back with New Eyes

This encounter marked the culmination of the healing process I had been in since I started ministry school. The deep pain and torment I had lived with for so long were finally and truly lifted from my heart and mind, and the experience of wholeness and freedom was completely exhilarating. But I soon discovered that God had an incredible gift waiting for me on the other side of surrender—the gift I had cried out for for so long.

For so long in that healing process, I had held God at a distance with the demand that He answer my questions about the past. What I didn't know was that answers weren't what I needed in my unhealed state. Answers would not heal my broken heart or restore my ability to trust. Only His love could do that. So even if He had given me answers, they wouldn't have satisfied what my heart needed. Only after He had healed me and restored my ability to trust could He give me answers—give me His truth about my story.

And so, through that healing encounter, God gave me new eyes—new eyes that could see my past through *His* eyes. Now, as I stood on the other side of surrender, He wanted to bring me into even greater strength and wholeness by rewriting my story from a place where I was connected to His heart and His love for me.

During times of prayer in the weeks and months following that encounter, the Lord led me back to the pivotal events of my life and began to show me His perspective on them. With every memory that He showed me, He answered the two big questions I had always asked Him: "Where were You?" and "Why did You let this happen?" First He showed me that He was always right there with me, and not as a passive observer, simply allowing things to unfold. He was protecting me, weeping with me, comforting me, and strengthening me. Then He showed me His redemptive purpose—which encompasses the end from the beginning—in even the most painful and confusing moments. In the process, He revealed certain truths about me that completely changed the way I saw my story and myself. It's incredible how different your story is when you look at it with Jesus.

A Fighter with a Voice

When Jesus took me back to my memories of my dad's first motorcycle wreck, I saw a beautiful gift inside a tiny girl make its first appearance. I watched as two-year-old Kim spoke to her dad in a coma and the room began to change. The Bible says our battles are "not against flesh and blood," but "against the spiritual forces of evil in the heavenly realms" (Ephesians 6:12). In that moment, there was a battle. The enemy was trying to steal my dad's life. He was fighting for it, and heaven was fighting on my dad's behalf. My voice called out to him and brought strength, encouraging him to fight. The gift that Jesus put inside me to bring breakthrough was doing just that. Even small children can partner with heaven to see the will of our Father done.

"The anointing you carry is not found in the songs you sing," Jesus told me. "It was put inside of you when I made you, and it is carried in your voice."

I cried when I realized that God, who does not exist within time like us, saw everything. He knew what would happen to my dad before I was even born. He knew how it would affect each of us, and He placed a gift inside me, not only to help my dad but also to help carry me to my own breakthrough.

I saw the same gift and fighting spirit emerge in the face of my first stepdad's hatred. Whether Peter knew it or not, the evil in him recognized Jesus in me and hated Him. I saw a fierce, five-year-old girl with a strong voice who wasn't afraid to say no and speak up when something wasn't right, and a big sister who fought to protect her little sister. Again Jesus put inside me what I needed. He was there, every moment, standing tall with me, fighting with me, and weeping with me. And again His voice whispered reminders in my ears: "You are strong. Use your voice. There is strength in your voice. I am with you."

When Jesus took me back to my years with Greg, it surprised me that I could see the glory and redemption even in this story. I saw the prayers of my grandparents commanding angels to surround us and fight on our behalf. And I saw a little girl who refused to be broken or allow her voice to be silenced. Jesus reminded me that I used to go in my room at night, turn on my music in my little cassette player (my favorite was Whitney Houston), and sing my heart out. He showed me that even in that moment as I listened to pop music, He was there with me, loving every minute of my singing and encouraging me to never stop.

I also saw that Jesus provided moments of peace and safety for me in the midst of the long battle. Even the one year spent by the ocean seemed to be a gift. Every time I looked outside my window and saw the ocean waves, I felt so much peace and happiness deep down in my soul. It was as if God created the ocean just to give me a beautiful view and bring me comfort. Never mind that it was only one year—it was just the boost I needed. The freezing winter when we lost our heat and electricity was also a gift, because I didn't have to endure certain difficult things I was experiencing at school at the time.

And the relief—the sweet, amazing relief—when Greg left! To this day, I have no idea why he decided not to come back, and I don't need to know either. When I looked at that memory, I saw the heart of ten-year-old Kim finally resting after a long battle, while Jesus stood close by, keeping guard while I carried the same confidence that He had built into my DNA the exact things I needed to endure the battles that lay ahead—a fighting spirit that wouldn't accept defeat and big emotions that caused me to love fiercely, stand up for what is right, and stay loyal to the end.

It felt so wonderful to be so known. Though I could talk all day about explanations and excuses for the poor choices of these men, in the end, their decisions, the plan of the enemy, and the abuse still did not stop God from loving me and meeting me. It didn't take away from His plan for my life, and it didn't change the fact that He created me and that I belong to Him.

A Pure Heart and a Great Purpose

Jesus also took me back to the memory of the woman who stopped me from worshiping in church, and my mom telling me I needed to know when to stop. Through my new eyes, I saw that everything I had believed about that experience had been a lie. Jesus didn't see a little girl putting on a show for attention, but one who was full of pure intention as she sang and danced in total and complete surrender, pouring love and adoration out to Him. Her innocent heart had been ignited with the hope of a future. I could see the joy on the Father's face as His little girl worshiped Him.

Everything I had felt, hoped, and believed in that moment about God's love and His purposes for my life had been real, but the lie of shame had led me to cast it aside. When I realized what had been stolen in that moment, it broke me. How different could my life have been if the woman hadn't sat me down? How different could my relationship with God have been if I had not been overcome by shame, embarrassment, and anger?

Thankfully Jesus gently reminded me that with Him, nothing is wasted. Tempted as I was to see myself as lost because of one moment, He never saw me as lost. I was His from the very beginning, and no amount of shame, anger, or pain could destroy what God had placed deep inside me. A fresh conviction of His sovereignty and the power of His redemption in my life settled deep in my heart.

Jesus also showed me the spiritual stakes of this whole experience and its consequences. Through my embarrassing experience with the woman, the enemy had been trying to attack three things in my life—my calling, my identity, and my relationship with the church.

When I sang "Amazing Grace" in the talent show, the gift I carry in worship made its first appearance, and a huge part of who I am as a worship leader was birthed. I surrendered to God in hunger and desperation, experienced an encounter and breakthrough moment with Him, and then shared it with others, leading them into their own moment of surrender and breakthrough in worship—the very pattern that has played out again and again throughout my life and ministry. I still remember opening my eyes after I sang and seeing people crying and being moved into worship. Likewise, when I stepped into worship at church the next Sunday, I knew I was doing what I had been created and called to do.

Knowing this, the enemy wanted nothing more than to shut down my gift and keep me from living in a place of surrender to God. He engineered an attack in which I felt humiliated for being "out of control" and unprotected by the One who had opened that vulnerable place of love and longing in my heart in the first place. The pain of humiliation was so intense that it made me want never to be out of control or vulnerable again. I numbed my emotions to stop the pain—at the price of silencing my gift and calling.

But the gifts and callings God places inside us are irrevocable, and there is no force on earth or in heaven that could come against or stop His love. Though the enemy wanted me to stay a scared and wounded little girl, God had set a plan into motion before any of these circumstances came about. I saw that He had been there in the moment of that painful attack, feeling my pain, yet full of strength and determination as He steadfastly covered the seeds He had planted deep inside my heart, fought for the gifts He had placed in me in my mother's womb, and looked ahead to the worship I would one day offer Him on the other side of this long battle. Even when I believed He was not protecting me, He was.

Jesus wasn't just protecting me and my gift for my own sake, however, but also for the sake of those whom these gifts would serve—members of His body. This was the enemy's other objective in attacking me—to cause pain through another believer, lead me to mistake them for my enemy, and get me to choose a path of isolation, mistrust, and distance with the church. This is a tactic he has used repeatedly in my life, as he does with all of us. Recognizing my true enemy made it much easier for me to forgive the woman for her misguided actions.

As important as it was for me to forgive her, however, the person I needed to forgive most was myself. When I was able to do that, it finally broke the power of that shame I had listened to in that experience. That was what enabled me to stop punishing myself for my rage and let my walls of self-protection come down at last.

Forgiving myself also broke the lid off the box of insignificance and purposelessness that shame had forced me to live in for so long. After my encounter with Jesus at the church camp, my first thought was that I wanted to do "something big" for Jesus. Dreaming and thinking big, as well as a desire for significance, flowed out of me naturally. As a child I had even dreamed of becoming the first woman president! But the enemy's lies had shut all that down. Later, when I was a teen, he had used the moment my mom said it wasn't my job to take care of her to double down on making me believe that my life had no purpose or value and lead me further down the path of isolation and self-destruction.

At one point when I was in high school, some ministers visited our church. In the meeting, they called up different people and prayed and spoke truth over them. One of the ministers called me up and said to me, "It is very important to the heart of God to tell you and to make sure you know that you matter. You matter." He said it over and over.

At the time I hadn't yet fully committed my life to Jesus, and I didn't fully understand how deeply my heart cried out to feel like I mattered and had some importance and significance to the world—but, more importantly, to God. When the Lord healed my heart, I understood that this was a cry He Himself had put in me.

The enemy had recognized it and attacked it, but in the end, God's purpose in my life couldn't be stopped. It didn't matter that I was banned from high school choir. Big whoop! My destiny was set at the foundations of time, and nothing can stop what God has set into motion and what God has put inside me. I could see that little girl who danced and sang then grew into a teen who performed in pageants, sang the anthem at football games, sang with her mom at church, and moved people to tears and worship every time she sang from her heart. I could see the power of that breakthrough anointing coming out as I shouted over my dad as he lay in a hospital bed. I could see the courage and strength God built into my DNA as I cared for my mom while she fought for her life. And I could see that this passion for worship was something that God placed in me from the beginning.

Chapter 6 | MY FIRST WORSHIP TEACHER

The journey of learning to see my identity and my past through a new lens, through God's perspective, was the beginning of true transformation in my life. And one of the first insights I was given as I began to live out of these new beliefs was that He also wanted to change the lens through which I viewed and related to other people—particularly my family. I discovered that a person misses a lot when they grow up seeing family members through the distortion of dysfunction, anger, and pain. After I was set free from those things, I was able to see truths about the people who were closest to me that I had never seen before. And the most surprising truth of all was seeing that the one family member I had pushed away most was the one whom God wanted to use to demonstrate His love to me in a way no other person in my life had.

As a child I never really felt angry with my mom. I saw her as a victim, just like myself. It wasn't until she had fully moved on with George that I felt upset with her. I was jealous that she could so easily leave the past behind while I felt trapped in it, unable to move forward. As I became healed and set free, I was able not only to forgive her but also to open my heart to her. It took a lot of time, but we eventually reached a place of deeper relationship and connection. With new eyes, I could see the fierce determination and strength it took for my mom to keep going. I could also see how strong she was to have endured the cruelty and trauma. I could see her devoted love for us and the way she made time to play with us and have some fun. It became apparent that my mom had many times laid down her own ambitions and needs to take care of ours. She had found a way to look after us, even when she was very young and probably very afraid and uncertain.

When we were little girls, I saw my sister Amy as an innocent and somewhat helpless child I was responsible to protect, and we were pretty much inseparable. Once we reached middle school and high school, however, we began coping with the pain of our traumatic childhoods in different ways. I watched as she embraced George more easily than I did, making me feel that, like Mom, she was moving on without me. As a result, I distanced myself from her, and we struggled to get along.

After I worked through my healing and began moving toward my sister, I discovered that she too was on a journey of healing. Through my healed lens, I saw that Amy was the only person in the world who had gone through the same things as me and felt the same pain as me. I saw that she had a strength inside of her too, which she wasn't even fully aware of yet. I saw how tender her heart was, as well as the gift of nurturing that God put inside her and protected. We both started to be vulnerable with each other and share the pain and brokenness we were processing, and thanks to that time of reconnection, we became best friends and bonded deeply and forever through our shared experiences and healing journeys.

George was a different story. When he married my mom, I had made George my enemy. I was certain he would fail us and hurt us, and I refused to open my heart to that kind of pain ever again. As George began to do things that made me happy, I fought the temptation to change my beliefs about him. The thought that he could be a good guy was even scarier to me than believing him to be a bad guy, because it required me to risk opening my heart to being loved by him.

Only on the other side of my healing encounter did I finally begin to see and accept that George was a friend and father who loved me, and someone whom I loved. In fact, as I looked back after my integration healing at the time George came into our lives, I began to acknowledge that not only was he not the bad guy in the story; he was the hero.

Generous Love

George adopted my baby brother, Matt. After Greg, Matt's biological dad, had disowned him, I was both relieved and scared for my brother. He was only two years old, but he understood what had happened, and it was very apparent that he was in pain. For a long time, any time we mentioned "Dad" or "Greg," Matt would clench his little fists and shout, "Don't say that word. I hate that word!" Then he would grunt and hold his breath with a look of anguish, his little cheeks turning from bright red to almost purple, until we shouted at him to breathe before he passed out. We tried wrapping our arms around him and loving him in those moments, but it didn't seem to help. He couldn't verbalize everything that had happened, but he knew and felt the rejection.

I remember the day Matt, at only two and a half years old, came to us and announced, "George is my new daddy now." George wasn't even married to my mom yet, but Matt had already made up his mind. A couple of years into the marriage, the adoption became final, and Matt received a new last name. It meant so much to me to know that my brother would have a very different life than I had. Matt and I have always been very close—I was more like a second mama to him than a sister. I felt so incredibly thankful to George for adopting him and taking care of him.

After my sister and I both graduated from high school and moved to California, George wanted to do fun things with Matt almost every weekend. I called Matt regularly to see how he was doing, and on one occasion, I heard a very disappointed-sounding Matt on the phone. I asked him what was wrong. He said, "Well, Mom and Dad want to take me four-wheeling at the dunes this weekend."

"Um . . . wow, Matt, that sounds like such a bummer," I said, my voice full of sarcasm. "What are you going to do?"

"I don't want to go with them," he whined. "They are *so* old!"

I burst out laughing and said, "Kid, you have no idea how good you have it!" And I was so happy that he had it so good.

George was just as loving and generous with Amy and me. He loved country music and dancing and used to take us to the Bum Steer Dance Palace, a Christian-owned country dance place in our little farm town, to learn the two-step and line dances. He bought my sister and me button-up shirts with tassels, bolo ties, cowgirl hats, and boots and made us feel like rodeo princesses on the dance floor.

Every once in a while, George would pick us up from school on a Friday and surprise us with a weekend trip to a waterslide park or some other fun place. Best of all, every summer he arranged a clothes shopping trip for "his girls" that made us absolutely giddy with excitement. He would book a suite at a fancy hotel, usually right next to a shopping mall, and let us order anything we wanted from room service for breakfast. We thought it was the most amazing thing to have a giant stack of pancakes and bacon delivered to our room door and eat them in bed. After breakfast, George gave each of us a wad of cash and sent us to the mall to pick out new clothes for the upcoming school year. To teenage girls who had gone through so much hardship, it felt like a dream come true.

George loved sports and encouraged me to participate, happily providing new shoes and equipment for each sport I chose. Despite my caution toward him, something in me still wanted to please him and gain his acceptance, so I did my best to excel in this area. Track was probably my best sport—I ran hurdles— and George was never shy about cheering for me at my meets. I also started taking golf lessons and joined a putting team at school as the only girl, winning our competition at the end of the year. My senior year, I played on Mom and George's team in a golf tournament and ended up winning "closest to pin" for the women. George, who was an avid golfer, was unbelievably proud of me and made such a big deal out of it. I tried to stuff down how happy it made me to make him proud, but it truly did.

Unfortunately I didn't have the same success in basketball. A tall beanpole of a girl, I was constantly tripping on my own feet and falling over. It didn't take much for someone to bump me and send me flying—my freshman coach ended up nicknaming me "Mop" because I was always on the floor! George would laugh until tears came out of his eyes, but he kept cheering me on nonetheless.

George was faithful to get up early every morning and spend time in prayer and worship. Every now and then, I would secretly listen in on his prayers, and one of the things he always prayed was, "Thank You for my girls." He usually had tears streaming down his face.

I couldn't understand why he was so thankful for me and why it made him so emotional. In fact, it made me angry. Due to my experiences with my other stepdads, I had come to believe I was unworthy of love, and it was painful to hear that I might be wrong, much as I wanted to be. For the same reason, it made me mad when George would randomly come to me and tell me how much he loved me and how proud of me he was. I usually rolled my eyes and walked away or made some smart remark. I didn't want to love him or feel happy with him, and I especially did not want to believe or feel his love for me. I felt that to do those things would leave me vulnerable to pain again.

What No Man Had Ever Done

Over and over, George disproved my negative beliefs about him. I kept waiting for him to be the villain and even tried to bring it out of him. I was constantly cold and rude to him, even cruel. I made it clear that I didn't trust him, didn't need him, and was just waiting for him to disappoint me. But even the one time I thought he finally proved me right about him—about four years into his marriage with my mom—didn't turn out the way I expected.

It happened one night when my cocker spaniel, who slept with me every night, woke me up barking and whining to be let out. As I opened my bedroom door, I heard the faint sound of voices arguing. Groggy as I was, it took me a moment to realize the voices were coming from Mom and George's bedroom. I quietly walked down the hallway and pressed my ear against their door to listen. After a few seconds, I thought I heard my mom cry out, "You're hurting me!"

This is it, I thought. *George has shown his true colors.*

I burst through the door and saw the two of them standing there. George had his hands on my mom's shoulders, and she was crying.

"Don't touch her!" I screamed, lunging at George.

George started to come toward me, but my mom jumped between us and shoved me out of the room, yelling, "Kim, stop! It's okay—everything is okay!"

I didn't believe her for one second. I ran back to my room to grab the baseball bat I kept underneath my bed for this very reason. As I turned to rush back with it, George stormed past me down the hall and out toward the front door. He was clearly angry, but he also seemed embarrassed. I had such a rush of emotions that I was not seeing clearly or taking the time to find out what was going on. My fear had instantly triggered me back into the little girl again who felt she needed to protect her family. I followed him, yelling, "You better not come back!" until I heard the door slam. I returned to my mom, who was sobbing.

"Kim, you don't understand," she repeated through tears, pleading with me. "Everything was okay. It wasn't what it looked like."

I refused to listen. What I had witnessed seemed very clear to me. I stayed up the rest of the night clutching my bat in case George came back, my mind racing with memories of past experiences.

The next morning, my mom had to force me to go to school. I didn't want to leave her. I kept telling her over and over, "See? I was right! He is just like the rest!" But she didn't respond.

When I got home from school that day, I found my mom, George, and the pastors of our church sitting in the living room.

"Will you sit down, Kim?" my mom asked.

As soon as I complied, all the thoughts in my head—all my fury at George and fear for my mom—began bursting out of my mouth.

"I knew you would hurt us! What you did to my mom is not okay!" I shouted at him. "I am not going to allow it. I will fight back! You are just like all the rest!"

I reveled in being right about him. I thought we were finally going to get rid of him, and I wouldn't have to deal with any stepdads ever again.

George sat listening and weeping through my tirade. And then he did the unthinkable, something I never saw coming.

"Kim, you are right," he said, his voice broken. "I hurt your mom and I hurt you, and it is not okay. I never should have done that." He looked directly into my eyes, grief clearly written on his face. "I am so, so sorry. Will you forgive me?"

He went on to explain that he had been reacting to his own wounds and had taken it out on us. He was horrified that he had scared us and hurt our feelings. I found out some time later that a minister had come to town and singled George out. He was praying for George and shared with him what he felt like God was saying. Whatever it was that this minister said, it connected to a deep wound in George's past. God was wanting to bring healing to George, and just like me, he was having a hard time facing it. On the night of his outburst, he and my mom had been discussing it all, and something had triggered George and sent him spinning.

"I promise you—and you have my full commitment forever—that I will never do anything like this again," he continued. "I will never hurt your mom or you kids again or cause you to become afraid of me. And if you will let me, I want to earn your trust again."

I was stunned. No man had ever done this. Neither of the stepdads had ever taken responsibility for what they did and apologized. Neither had ever vowed never to hurt me in that way again.

I didn't know what to say—it was as if my brain was short-circuiting. Unable to come up with a meaningful response, I just quietly said, "Okay. I forgive you."

George responded with humility and gratitude. He reached out his hand to touch me, but I know he could feel my walls and see that I wasn't quite ready for an embrace.

I walked away still feeling angry, but also disarmed. Instead of getting rid of George, I had let him come just a tiny bit closer.

Unwavering and Unrelenting

As I looked back at the memory of George's apology from a healed place, I couldn't help but cry. Becoming more whole allowed me to feel love for George and see his good intentions toward me. Clearly that night's incident was not a good representation of who he was. Honestly, I didn't even know what to think about it, and I wanted to put it behind me forever. But Jesus wanted me to see something else in this memory—that in apologizing and repenting, George had done something no other man had ever done in my life. Jesus wanted me to see that George was a man of humility and integrity, and that he never stopped pursuing my heart. His request for forgiveness had formed a crack in the dysfunctional foundations built through my past, and over time, that crack had spread, giving me hope that his heart toward me—and the Father's heart too—were good.

Once again I saw God in my story. He had sent George to us. I am convinced that I am a Christian today because of George and the way he brought God and church into our lives. Because of him, church went—from my perspective—from being a ritual to being a pillar of our family culture. If George had not come into our lives, changing the course we were on, I don't know for certain that I would be who I am today and have the relationship with Jesus that I have.

God not only brought a man to love my mom the way she had always desired to be loved, but He brought a father to show us the unrelenting love of Jesus. Even though I rejected him from the beginning, George never wavered in his love for me. It didn't seem to matter how many hurtful things I said or did. When I pushed him away, he still moved toward me. Even when I didn't respond, he still told me how special I was and that he loved me as if I were his own. I didn't believe I was special or beautiful or worthy of love, but George told me I was anyway.

As I looked back at all the ways George had loved me, fought for me, protected me, provided for me, and cared for me, I saw Jesus and His relentless pursuit of me. George was an incredible example of the way Jesus will stop at nothing to show us His love. Jesus was there from the very beginning. He was there in the moments of pain and heartache, anger and questioning. When I put my heart on lockdown, Jesus did not step back or grow tired in fighting to set it free. Throughout my journey of being integrated and healed, parts of me would hide my heart away and in anger not allow Jesus to come near. But every time I came back to my next meeting with the counselor, there He would be again. It seemed that no matter how many times I was angry with Him or rejected Him, He always responded when we prayed and turned our attention to Him. When I pushed Him away and rejected His kindness, He kept showering me with all His goodness anyway. It is truly amazing the way Jesus has loved me.

It was also profound to realize that God is not obligated to love me the way I think He should. He loves me in the way I need it most, which is sometimes in a way I don't see. As a parent, I do not take pleasure in disciplining my children, but I do it because I love them so much and want them to be healthy, happy, safe, and respectful humans who love and contribute to society.

God may withhold things from my life, but it is not to punish me or hurt me. It is because He loves me and wants to protect me. I truly believe that even the most broken person, if they are willing, can look back at their life and find a moment in which God was loving them. We just don't always see it when we are in the thick of it. I didn't think it was loving of God to send George into our lives—I didn't even believe God had done that at all. But it was exactly what I needed. George was essential to my life and all I was created to do.

As I look back now at all the special and fun memories with George, I realize that God was restoring some of my childhood. I hadn't seen it at the time. I was so wrapped up in what I had been robbed of. I told my mom I couldn't move on and had no idea how to be a kid and just enjoy life, but that is exactly what was happening. The fun trips, the shopping, the sporting events, the dancing, the water fights—all of it gave me back part of my childhood. George brought a joy and security that allowed me to live carefree. When children feel safe, they are their happiest. They let down their walls and live it up without any shame or fear. I was feeling safe for the first time in my life, and I couldn't even acknowledge it.

When I realized I had missed this, shame and guilt tried to rush in, but Jesus addressed it and shut it down instantly. "You didn't see it with your eyes and your mind back then, but your heart and your spirit caught it and felt it," He told me. "I'm showing you this now not to make you feel bad, but to show you that even then I was working on your behalf and moving you toward freedom."

The Bible says we love God because He first loved us. It is very simple. If you don't love Him, if you aren't passionate about pursuing Him, it is because you don't know yet how much He loves you. When you feel and hear and see the love of God, you cannot help but respond with love.

That is the true beauty of this part of the story. George kept pouring out love, and I finally learned to love him. The safety and joy he brought enabled me to recover some of my childlike ability to love and trust again. Meanwhile, Jesus never stopped pursuing my heart and loving me through it all until I surrendered my heart and love to Him.

The last thing Jesus pointed out in my healing journey as we went through these memories together was the way George worshiped Him. Witnessing George faithfully getting up so early every morning to read his Bible, pray, and sing to Jesus was my first exposure to worship outside church. It was my first revelation that you could have a relationship with Jesus and that our connection to God does not exist solely inside the walls of the church. It was the first time I had seen what it looked like to pursue God in our home. My mom loved to play the piano and sing (those are special memories to me), but there was something different and powerful about seeing a man—the leader in our family—being so vulnerable and establishing an environment of peace in our home.

I had never seen so much passion and worship poured out in a moment at home and not in a church service. I realized I had grown up with a belief that God was little more than a story and that any evidence of His presence and reality resided within a church. I hadn't realized that He desires a relationship with me, that I should desire a relationship with Him, or that a real relationship was even attainable.

George's faithfulness to this was seared in my mind, and when I finally surrendered my life to Jesus in high school, I knew what to do. I did it without even thinking about it. I began to pull away alone, read my Bible, pray, and sing to Jesus. When I left home to go to college and ministry school, I naturally continued to do these things. George instilled in me an image of what passionate worship looked and sounded like—a person completely lost in adoration and surrender to Jesus, unashamed of tears and unconcerned about what anyone thought.

It's fascinating that these things would go on to be some of the characteristics that have marked my life and who I am as a worship leader. Even as a teen when I was sorting through who I thought God was and my connection to Him, George was planting seeds deep inside of me. Even more than the hero, more than the man sent to us by God, more than someone who helped bring restoration, George was one of my first teachers of true worship.

Chapter 7 | ABIDING TRUST

When Jesus asked me not to audition for the worship team at ministry school and not to tell people I sang, He told me He would bring singing back into my life, but in His way and in His time. He wanted me to spend that first year in school focused on inner healing, and my job was simply to keep my heart yielded to Him as He did a deep work inside me.

Meanwhile, I continued to volunteer as a leader in the youth group, helping Banning Liebscher, who was the youth pastor. I was really thankful to have a place to go every week where I felt safe, had friends, and could have a reprieve from dealing with all the rewiring happening inside me.

I was also really excited about the youth conference coming up in the summer. Banning had started "Jesus Culture" conferences in the summer of 1999 (the first one I attended was in 2001), and I was especially looking forward to the part of the conference where we took the kids out to the streets to do block parties. The plan was to take over a cul-de-sac in a low-income neighborhood; throw a big party complete with food, a bounce house, candy, and music; and share Jesus with the people who came. I couldn't wait!

Getting to Know "Holy Spirit"

Before that summer after my first year of ministry school, however, God asked me to do something that took me *way* out of my comfort zone. March was "missions month" at school, and every student was expected to go on a missions trip. There was an option to stay in Redding and do street ministry, which would have been my preference, but when I prayed about it, I felt that God was telling me to join the team going to Mozambique, Africa.

This was terrifying to me. In the two years I had lived in Redding, I had become a bit of a recluse. Perhaps it was the constant moving and change through my childhood, or maybe it was all the inner healing I was going through, that left me feeling very vulnerable, but in that season of my life, I was overwhelmed with fear at the idea of traveling. I wasn't interested in venturing out anywhere beyond my small world of ministry school, work, and church.

My good friend Jodi, who knew I preferred staying in hermit mode, once invited me to drive to the coast for a day with her. We both agreed it would be good for me to face my fears and get out of town. But soon after we began the drive into the mountains west of Redding, we had to pull over because I was so overcome by fear that I started hyperventilating! We decided to turn around and go back home.

So, the idea of going to Africa seemed about as crazy as traveling to the moon! Yet I could not shake that still small voice inside me encouraging me to go to Mozambique. I finally took a deep breath and signed up to go, thinking, *I might regret this.*

Miraculously God provided all the money I needed for my trip. Jodi, who had traveled extensively, helped me pack, and I was on my way. After more than twenty-four hours of travel, I arrived in Africa. Unfortunately my bag did not, which, in my mind, was possibly the worst thing that could happen to me. I was not like the other gung-ho ministry students on the trip, who acted like they were built for contingencies such as landing in a developing nation without their belongings. For three days we drove from the orphanage and missions base where we were staying to the airport to see if my bag had come in. The whole time, I couldn't help but wonder, *Am I being punished?* But on the third day, it finally arrived.

I had a very difficult time adjusting to Mozambique. My team was eager to go out to the bush and the dump to tell people about Jesus, bring medical aid, and pray for people. I didn't want to go anywhere. I wanted to stay within the confines of the base. I didn't even want to go into the orphanage where all the children were. My team became frustrated and even angry with me, wondering why I had even bothered to come if all I was going to do was sit inside the base. I wondered the very same thing. *Why am I here? Why did God ask me to come?* I couldn't do what everyone else was doing because it just didn't feel like me.

Then one day, my team leader asked if I could teach a group of ten-year-olds at the orphanage how to hear Jesus and pray for others. She explained that the whole team was leaving me behind to go on an overnight trip to the bush, so I was the only one available to visit the orphanage. Feeling like I didn't have much of a choice, I agreed.

The next morning I prepared my lesson and nervously followed a woman into the classroom where I was to teach. To my complete surprise, the kids eagerly absorbed everything I said.

At the end of the lesson, I told them I wanted us to practice what we had just learned. They paired up and began to pray for each other. They took the time to ask God what He wanted to say to the friend they were praying for and then courageously spoke it out.

As I looked around the room, I saw many children with tears streaming down their cheeks, clearly having an encounter with Jesus as truth was being spoken over them. Afterward, the schoolteacher who was there with me asked me to come the next day and teach again to a new group of students.

I ended up teaching twice more. Then all the teachers and leaders of the school got together and asked me to come teach them how to do what I had done. They wanted to keep teaching the kids how to communicate with God and grow in their relationship with Him. The way I had done it was so effective, they said, that they wanted to know how to do it themselves. My team continued to go out and do the things they loved, while I stayed back and taught the kids, helped take care of babies in the nursery, and prepared hot meals for the team to enjoy when they returned.

One day while I was praying, I felt the Lord showing me that this whole trip to Mozambique was about me getting familiar with Holy Spirit and learning to listen and to follow His guidance in my life. The opportunity to teach people in a foreign country what I had learned helped me see and own how much He had been teaching me about how to hear and trust Him! This trip is where a true friendship with Him began in my life. From that point on, I have referred to Him as "Holy Spirit," rather than "the Holy Spirit." It feels so formal to put "the" in front of my Friend's name.

The trip to Africa stretched me in ways I couldn't have anticipated. It woke me up to the inner healing work God was doing inside me. When the Jesus Culture conference rolled around, I had even more confidence and boldness in helping to lead the youth in following Holy Spirit as they went out and did street ministry. Even while He had me under construction, I was becoming more and more on fire for others to know and encounter Him.

Unlocking Worship

When my second year of ministry school began, I felt God tell me He was going to bring singing back into my life but reminding me to wait for Him and His perfect timing.

A couple of months later, in early December, I was standing in the back of one of the classrooms when the worship pastor walked by. He stopped, got a funny look on his face, and walked back over to me. "Do you want to sing?" he asked.

With wide eyes, I said, "Yes."

"Good," he said. "Go look at the schedule posted on the wall and see when I'm leading next. You can sing with me."

I knew this had to be some sort of miracle. I didn't know a single leader in ministry who would walk up to a stranger and ask them to jump on the stage with them. I walked over to the posted schedule to see when he was leading next, and to my complete surprise it was December 19—my birthday! What a gift! I could almost see Jesus' face with a giant grin on it.

In addition to singing backup on Sunday mornings, I started singing with the worship bands for the school of ministry and youth group. However, I quickly discovered that stepping on stage didn't automatically mean stepping into freedom and confidence as a worship leader. When I watched my friend Chris Quilala, whom I had met when I first came to youth group while attending Simpson, lead the youth worship team at our weekly gatherings and at the summer Jesus Culture conference, I saw a level of ease and comfort in the leadership position that I just didn't have yet.

I preferred singing backup because I could hide to some degree. The first time I was asked to lead a song for a Sunday morning main service, I completely messed up in the middle of it, ran off the stage sobbing, and swore I would never do it again. But I felt Jesus urging me to keep trying to grow as a worship leader, asking, "Do you trust Me?"

One of my struggles was that I felt so much reverence for God and didn't want to deface worship with any kind of selfish ambition or performance. How was I to keep completely focused on God while standing on a stage under bright lights in front of thousands of people? This felt like a huge problem for me, especially because I always felt such deep passion bubbling in my spirit and longing to emerge in worship. I was afraid that if I let all that passion out, I would not only make a fool of myself, but also somehow defile what felt so sacred to me. I was scared to have another moment like the one in my childhood when I "didn't know when to stop." *What if I get so passionate in worship that I offend people?* I kept trusting my leadership and taking steps forward, but I had a lot of uncertainty.

After my integration healing happened toward the end of my second year of ministry school and the power of the lies from the past was broken, I started stepping into a new level of freedom in every area of life, including leading worship. When ministry school ended, I decided to remain in Redding and continue working as a nanny, helping Banning with the youth group and the summer Jesus Culture conferences, and singing on the worship team whenever I was scheduled or asked.

Though I had already completed two years of counseling, I decided to start seeing a new counselor to help me as I stepped into this new season of wholeness and growth. I recognized that many of the ways I had learned to interact with people and respond to situations in childhood were unhealthy and needed to be replaced, so I discussed various situations or problems popping up in my life with my counselor, and he coached me through effective ways to communicate, make my needs known, draw boundaries, and respond. I loved learning and growing and felt very happy to be in such a healed place.

However, there was something even deeper that I needed to learn to walk in—a new habit of believing, thinking, and behaving that governed all these healthy relational behaviors I was trying to learn. I needed to learn to live out consistent, abiding trust in Jesus. Though I had been learning to trust Him ever since I had given my life to Him in high school, and especially during the two years of ministry school, my childhood habits of self-protection were still deeply ingrained in my thinking and behavior.

It was one thing for those fractured parts, during a counseling session, to make the choice to surrender their job of self-protection and choose to trust Jesus to do it instead. It was another to learn how to build a lifestyle of trusting Him as I navigated the often scary and painful challenges and mysteries of life, ministry, and relationships. But I knew that if I was to live with a free heart and no walls, I would have to figure out how to do this. I also realized that despite surrendering, I still had a powerful need for control, which was going to be the real issue to work through.

Growing in this lifestyle of trust took time. There was no overnight transformation, just baby steps (and stumbling, falling, and getting back up again) to practice courage in being the new Kim—the confident leader, the vulnerable friend, and the trusting daughter who knew her Father wanted the gifts in her to come out and bless people. But with every choice to believe I was who He said I was, the more I became that person.

However, eventually I reached a point, as I neared the end of my fourth year in Redding, where I felt God stirring something in my heart. As I prayed and talked to Him about it, I realized that the passion I longed to express in worship was still locked up inside me—*and He wanted it to come out*. He also showed me that it would not be unlocked in Redding—the keys were not in this church or in this city.

This meant a transition was coming. I would need to leave the place that had become so familiar and comfortable. However, whenever I prayed about this transition and felt sure that God was telling me it was time to move on, I never got a clear picture of where or to what He was calling me. Questions plagued me. *What if I'm wrong? What if I decide to leave and then miss out on something amazing or a really great opportunity? What if I make a wrong choice and end up somewhere that makes me miserable?* After all the hills of trust I had summited in the previous four years, it felt like God had now led me to a mountain, and I didn't know if I was ready to start climbing.

Pennies and Promises

It's so easy to become stuck and somewhat frozen in time when you aren't getting a clear word from God about what's next, only a prompting in your heart to keep walking. I saw others in my own circle of friends who also felt they were supposed to do something different but didn't know what, and who then allowed fear to just keep them standing still. As I pondered this and talked to Jesus about it during my devotional times, I began to hear His still small voice whispering to my heart, "Step out. You can trust Me."

The Lord began to remind me of story after story from the previous few years in which I could see the faithfulness of God and trust His voice inside me. One of my favorites was the time my phone broke during my second year of ministry school.

I was living in a small, second-floor apartment with a friend who was also attending the school. We both worked part-time jobs because of our school schedule, and I struggled to make ends meet, often supplementing my groceries with donations from the church pantry. I had a landline telephone that I used to stay connected to my family, usually calling collect. One day I picked up my phone and realized it wasn't working. I knew I had paid the bill. I unplugged it and plugged it back in, but it wouldn't turn on. Feeling hopeless, I started crying. It was my only means of communication with my family, and I couldn't afford to replace it.

Suddenly I felt Holy Spirit show me a picture. I saw inside the body of the phone, and I saw myself inserting a penny into a very particular spot. *What a weird picture!* Deciding I had nothing to lose, I grabbed a penny and opened the phone. The wires and various electronic components looked just like what I had seen in my mind. I saw the spot where I needed to slide the penny. I slid it in carefully and then put the phone back together, set it on the base, took a deep breath, and held up the receiver to my ear. A dial tone! It worked—and that phone never had a problem again. To this day, I have no idea why the penny worked. All I know is that God proved He can be trusted to bring solutions to my problems. He loves to take care of me.

Another story God reminded me of was the time I had budgeted all my money, down to the last cent, and had seventy dollars of food money for an entire month. As I was driving to school, I saw a haggard-looking man standing on the side of the road, holding a sign announcing he needed food for his family. I felt convicted to do something and decided I wanted to help him. I pulled over and asked him if I could buy him groceries. He said yes, so I told him to get in my car and I would drive him to the grocery store right up the road. (Side note: my mom hates this part of the story! *What was I thinking? A young, single girl inviting a strange man into her car?* I was trying to focus on following the voice of Jesus, but this should include the voice of wisdom too!)

When we went into the grocery store, the man grabbed a cart, went straight to the baby section, and picked out a small package of diapers, formula, and baby food. Then he went and got milk, meat, and a few cans of soup. My heart broke to think that he had a baby he was struggling to feed and was in a position to need this help. When I paid for the items in his cart, the total came to seventy dollars—all the money I had. After we walked out, I prayed for him, and he thanked me over and over, with tears streaming down his face. Only when I drove away to school did I start to wonder how I was going to eat that month.

After class that day, I got home to find a message on my answering machine from my grandma. "Hi Kim! Papa and I were praying for you today, and we felt like we were supposed to deposit some money in your bank account. So we went down to the bank and deposited seventy dollars into your account. We love you!"

I burst into tears. My Jesus, the One who doesn't abandon me, had again taken such good care of me.

More stories filled my mind as I thought about trusting God. It was almost as if God was asking, "Have I not proven Myself faithful?"

It was this history of His faithfulness that finally gave me the courage to leave Redding. A few people in my church didn't think it was a great idea, but I stuck to my guns. I was determined to trust Jesus and step out into unknown waters. I was ready for something to shift inside of me.

Finding the Spontaneous

In the end, God stirred in my heart an awareness that it was time to leave, but He let me decide where to go first. I chose to move back to Oregon to live with my grandparents, who lived in a town near my biological dad. I hadn't yet gotten to spend quality time getting to know him on the other side of healing, like I had with the other members of my family, and I wanted to do that.

I got a part-time job at a retail store, and I loved being with my grandparents again. I visited my dad and attended a local church, where I made a couple of friends. It didn't seem like anything significant was happening—but I felt peace. God was with me and doing something inside me, and I decided I didn't need to understand it all. I was doing my best to relinquish my need for control and just let Him be God in my life. It seemed that perhaps this time was not about "doing" as much as it was about just "being." It was a nice reprieve from all the heart work and ministry I had been doing, and it was nice to spend some time with my dad while living from a more healed and whole place. This was a short season that seemed to quiet everything inside my mind and soul and make room for what was coming next.

After a few months in Oregon, I was ready to move on again. I wanted to go places where I had heard God was doing something amazing. I didn't know what I was looking for or what I needed—I just wanted to sit in those environments and see if God would do something amazing in me, particularly when it came to unlocking that thing inside me connected to worship.

I first went to Kansas City, where there is a ministry called the International House of Prayer. They have ongoing prayer and worship twenty-four hours a day, seven days a week. I sat in on a few different prayer sessions there. It was a special time with Jesus, but I felt like I was supposed to keep moving, so I headed to Charlotte, North Carolina. I had a friend there, Molly Williams, who led worship at a church called MorningStar Fellowship Church, and she invited me to stay for a while and join the worship team as a background singer.

At MorningStar I met a fellow worship leader and friend of Molly's named Suzy Wills (now Suzy Yaraei). Suzy was the freest person I had ever seen in my life. She was not only a talented vocalist, but she led worship with such deep passion, freedom, and sensitivity to Holy Spirit. Usually at some point during whatever song she was leading, she would burst into a spontaneous song, going completely off script. She didn't care what anyone thought, and she was determined to lead people into the same freedom she herself exuded.

I felt like most of the time I was onstage, I just watched Suzy with awe and wonder. *How does she just start singing something spontaneously, and it's exactly what needs to be said in the moment?* Watching and listening to her, it was very clear she had walked through the fire with Jesus many times and had a trust and love for Him that was unwavering. I could identify with her, almost as if we had similar scars. But I longed for the freedom she was walking in.

One evening I was singing background vocals with Molly and Suzy during a worship set when there was a momentary lull. The band was playing, but no one was singing. My heart started racing, and I could feel Molly's eyes burrowing into me! Suddenly her hand was on my back, gently pushing me forward as she said in her thick Southern accent, "Sing something. You got something."

All I could think was, *No, I do not.* I shook my head at her, eyes wide as saucers. But then I opened my mouth, and suddenly, from somewhere deep in my spirit, a song came out. The words just flowed out like it was a song that had been trapped inside for a long time. As the words came out, Molly and Suzy both started crying.

"You can have all of me," I sang. "You can have every part of me . . ."

It wasn't as though words appeared in my mind, causing me to read a script. It was more like a fountain had been turned on, and all I did was open my mouth to let it out. It was a bubbling up of heartfelt emotions, transformed into lyrics and melody.

Even the melody came out pretty easily. The band kept playing the same chord progression over and over, so that helped with anticipating where the music would go and then following it.

I could feel Jesus—His presence, pleasure, and excitement in that moment. And as the room responded to what was being sung, I could see the way Holy Spirit was using it to bring glory to Him. People were joining in with what I was singing, lifting their hands, crying, and singing out their own words to Jesus. It was as if we were all being swept away in the overflow of that fountain.

I had a lot of questions that night, and Molly and Suzy were happy to teach me, pray for me, and encourage me. They talked about the importance of the band staying on the same chord progression when you sing out spontaneously so that you can settle into a melody. They talked about how you can help bring breakthrough to a moment in worship when you step out boldly and lead in freedom. They also taught me how helpful it is to find phrases that can be repeated so that the people you are leading can catch on to them and sing along with you.

I knew I had stepped into something new that had forever changed me as a worshiper and worship leader. Suzy and Molly kept pushing me out of my comfort zone and encouraging me. Molly taught me how to have some backbone and jump out into the middle of a song with boldness. I learned it was okay to make mistakes, and nobody is expected to be perfect.

This is the beauty of worship. It's not a performance. It's just a bunch of God's kids coming together to worship Him. And like any loving father, He loves the affection and attention we give Him. I also learned how beautiful it is when I do engage my emotions. Suzy helped me see that I can express big emotions in worship and live outside of the box, just like Jesus. It was through watching Suzy that I could feel the painful memory of a little girl thinking she was "too much" because she "didn't know when to stop" fading away. On a scale of one to ten in freedom and expression, Suzy was always an eleven, and we all loved her for it. To this day I tell people that everything I learned about worship leading, I learned from Suzy and Molly during my season in Charlotte.

I had been gone from Redding for a bit more than a year when something inside me said it was time to go back. Whatever it was that had been locked up now felt open wide and ready for whatever Jesus was going to do. There was no checklist that had been completed or any accomplishment I could point to. It was just a feeling of being settled and of anticipation mixed together. I had stayed connected with Banning while I was away, and the Jesus Culture conference was ready to begin. He asked me if I would help Chris Quilala lead worship at it. I surprised myself by excitedly saying I would. My lack of fear proved that something had shifted in me.

That first time I led at Jesus Culture was eye-opening for everyone! A wild and untamed passion came surging out of me while leading. I was fearless and bold as I danced, sang, shouted, and held nothing back in worshiping Jesus. I wasn't afraid to address the crowd and encourage them to step out in freedom as well. And to my sheer delight, spontaneous worship just flowed out of me.

When I walked off the stage, so many people who had known me before I left said, "Kim, what happened to you?" Everyone could see and feel the change. It was hard to verbalize a response to their questions though. I had felt like I needed to be unlocked and went out in search of the key. Sure enough, something had opened up inside me on that journey, and I came home a different person. I was just as excited and confused about it as everyone else!

The more I stepped out in worship, boldly making declarations about what I felt God was doing in us and saying to us, the more my confidence and faith grew. I didn't fear mistakes, and spontaneously singing was becoming easier and easier. A new authority came with my new level of freedom. The passion and joy that came bursting out of me with every lyric ignited the hearts of those I was leading.

Once after a worship set, a lady came up to me and said, "We just needed permission." I realized that everything I had fought for became something into which I could lead others. They just needed to see passion in worship displayed to know what it could be. I learned to press through in worship toward greater freedom and breakthrough, and people would follow me there. I soon learned that all my private victories could be translated into communal victories as I led.

This journey of freedom, breakthrough, and authority in worship culminated, as I shared in the first chapter, with the recording of our first two albums and the video of "How He Loves" that went viral and changed everything for Jesus Culture. Invitations to lead worship at other churches and events began to pour in. Our sense of responsibility to honor and steward what God was giving us and doing through us led us to create our own record label, rather than signing with another label, to develop further projects and protect everything we were doing. We were not necessarily planning on recording many albums or bringing on other artists, but we loved doing ministry and wanted to continue pouring our hearts into our Jesus Culture conferences, which were now taking place all over the world.

Shortly after we released *We Cry Out*, I also released my first solo record titled *Here Is My Song*. It felt like a big achievement, as it contained five songs and five tracks that were just spontaneous worship, all recorded live—not a common thing at the time. Because of that, it drew a lot of attention, discussion, and excitement.

However, even as all this was happening, I didn't think leading worship would be my life or career. I had gotten a job as an entry-level teller at a bank when I moved back to Redding, worked my way up, and soon found myself selling loans as a banker. I was successful at my job, and I loved it. I loved the stability and safety of routine it provided.

I had evenings, weekends, and holidays off, and I was able to lead worship on the weekends at church. When invitations to lead worship elsewhere came up or a Jesus Culture conference took place in another city, I could usually take some time off to attend. I felt incredibly thankful for every opportunity, but I was so focused on continuing to become whole and healthy, walking in my newfound freedom, and growing my relationship with Jesus. He was my sole focus, and the only thing that mattered to me was staying connected to Him.

Thanks to my banking job, I was making more money than I ever had in my life, and I loved not having to worry about my bills and expenses. I thought maybe this would be my life and career. However, it didn't take long before God invited me into another journey of trust—this time through an uncharted part of my heart.

Chapter 8 | FIREWORKS

At this point in my life, most of my friends, including my sister, had gotten married and were having babies. I was happy in my career and worship leading. Some days, the idea of marriage terrified me; other days, it was something I really wanted. I questioned my ability to choose somebody and worried that I would make some of the mistakes my mom had made.

I started dating a guy, and I went on to date him off and on for a couple of years. I think I was drawn to him because he was quiet, mysterious, and an emotional artist. I had decided I wanted to marry someone whose parents hadn't divorced. I'd had enough divorce in my life and didn't want to marry into it. I felt selfish for thinking that way and wasn't sure I even deserved that, but it was a desire in my heart.

This guy's parents were still happily married, and I thought there was a lot of potential for us. However, as time went on, it became clear that our relationship was deeply unhealthy. He became more and more controlling, telling me how I should or shouldn't dress, that I shouldn't eat so much and should watch my weight, and—this one upset me the most—that I didn't understand how things should be in a relationship because of my upbringing. He also began to grow jealous of me and the opportunities that came my way. He told me that if I married him, I would need to make different music that was softer and not so loud and expressive.

His words slowly started to pull something out of me that had been hiding somewhere deep in a shadowy corner of my heart—self-hatred. I began to look in the mirror and think I looked ugly or too chubby. I hated that I laughed so loud and had such a big personality. A resounding message kept running through my mind: *you are too much.* My emotions were too big, and I had way too many of them. My expression of passion was too loud and too wild.

I began to struggle to stay connected to Jesus while I was in this relationship. It was as if I had allowed this guy's voice to become louder than Jesus' voice in my life. The self-hatred was feeding something even uglier—self-pity. I began to feel sorry for myself, as if I were powerless in this situation and stuck. I was believing lie after lie, unaware of the deeper spiritual assault on my life and identity.

Then one night I had a dream. I was walking toward what appeared to be a circus tent. Inside was a roller coaster with a big sign on the top that read, "Redemption Roller Coaster." When I entered the tent, a woman saw me and yelled, "Self-pity!" A slimy, pitiful-looking car rolled up out of a dark hole, and I got inside it and sat down. It started moving slowly down a rickety track into darkness. I could hear the words I had spoken over myself in self-pity, the lies I had believed.

Suddenly we were climbing up a steep hill. As we neared the top, I saw a doorway we were about to go through, and above it was written, "The Blood Room." The car peaked and went rushing down the track. As it raced around the room, both the car and I were being completely covered in red, and I realized it was the blood of Jesus. I could feel myself becoming clean, and I saw that the car was also transforming and becoming new. Then we started climbing again toward a bright light. When we came out on the other side into the light, I saw Jesus. He ran to me with a huge smile on His face and embraced me. I also saw many people all around us, cheering about the breakthrough that had just happened.

When I woke up from the dream, I started crying. I could feel the power of self-pity and self-hatred being broken off me, and in a moment, I had a revelation. I was doing what I had witnessed my mom doing. I was choosing a man who needed to be fixed. I was trying to save him and help him in some way, but in doing so, it was only tearing me down. I broke up with him that day and never looked back.

After that, the voice of self-hatred still tried to rise up from time to time, but I gained some tools to help me face that monster and send it back where it came from. One was to keep a journal in which I wrote down everything Jesus said about me—every encounter, every moment in His presence, and every encouraging word. When self-hatred or self-pity tried to speak, I went back and read the journal to remind myself of what He says about me.

The Right One

In 2007, I was asked to come on staff at Bethel as a worship pastor. Banning had been urging me to leave my job as a banker and step into ministry full-time for a while. I had become so comfortable in my job. To step into full-time ministry seemed like a big risk to me. But I took the leap of faith! As a worship pastor, I began scheduling worship teams, training and teaching team members, hosting small groups, and leading worship for all kinds of meetings and events. Meanwhile, our Jesus Culture albums continued to take off, and we kept recording. We began taking our conference to other cities and countries more frequently. I was busy growing, learning, and trusting Jesus—and loving every minute of it.

In July 2007, I gathered with some friends for a BBQ to celebrate Independence Day. The Fourth of July is my favorite holiday, and I absolutely love watching fireworks at night after a full day of hanging with my friends. But on that particular night, I looked around at all the couples around me watching the fireworks and felt alone. I told God I was thankful for my life, but that I sometimes wished I had someone to share it with. I felt like God suddenly responded and said, "The next time you watch the fireworks, you won't be watching them alone."

A year later, on the night of July 3, 2008, I went to watch a friend perform some original songs at a café, ended up getting food poisoning, and spent the rest of the night extremely sick, which forced me to cancel all my plans for the Fourth. I was devastated. I remembered what God had told me the year before, and I thought, *What a joke! I obviously didn't hear God say that. I must have made it up in my head.*

I was so mad. I was sick and alone on my favorite holiday! But then I turned on the TV and got a welcome surprise. The local news was reporting that the Fourth of July fireworks display had been postponed. Horrible forest fires had been burning on all the mountains surrounding Redding, filling the air with so much smoke that they couldn't do the fireworks show. I was relieved that I wouldn't miss them after all—and wondered about the *next* next time I would be watching them.

Even so, I was frustrated and discouraged that nothing had materialized over the previous year in the dating department. It had become harder and harder to maneuver as a single woman in a growing ministry. I had run into weird things—people who thought I wasn't allowed to be in ministry because I wasn't married, and single men who were convinced that God told them I was "the one." It was getting stickier and stickier to figure out who was interested in me for who I was and who was after the platform and making some sort of name for themselves.

That September, I went to Spokane, Washington, to lead worship for a conference. I had a friend who lived near the area, and we decided to meet for lunch. She told me she had invited a few other friends to join us, and when I got to the restaurant, there he was—Skyler Smith.

I knew Skyler from my elementary school years in Klamath Falls, Oregon. The first time I saw him was at a church youth camp, and I immediately fell into whatever love feels like at the awkward age of twelve or thirteen. I had even practiced writing "Mrs. Kimberlee Smith" and "I love Skyler Smith" in my diary.

The moment I saw him at lunch in Spokane for the first time in ten years, I felt the same attraction I'd had as a young girl. He looked like the same Skyler I had known as a kid—but the muscular, tall, dark, and handsome version. He had long curly hair that I could have easily been jealous of. When we were at lunch, I noticed that he still had a soft-spoken voice and gentle manner about him. I could feel the peace and steadfastness just oozing off of him. His confident demeanor was very attractive. I had no idea if he was married or had a girlfriend, but I was anxious to find out!

Despite the temptation to ignore everybody else at the table and just talk to Skyler, I played it cool until it was time to go. As everyone was leaving, I heard myself ask him, "Do you want to go for a walk and catch up?" It was like an out-of-body experience! *What did I just say?* I was so embarrassed and sure he thought the invitation was awkward and strange, but to my surprise, he eagerly said, "Yes!"

We walked to a nearby park and spent two hours talking about what we had been doing the previous ten years. It was apparent that we had been on very similar journeys. They looked different, but we had ended up in the same place. I definitely felt like there was a connection between us, and I was hoping he would ask for my number.

To my disappointment, however, we got through the whole conference and Skyler never asked for my number, email address, or any other way to contact me. I was so frustrated! Had I just imagined the connection between us? I thought about giving him my number anyway and saying, "Just in case," but something inside me made me put my foot down. I decided I was going to be pursued, no matter what, and wouldn't settle for anything less. If he wanted me, he would have to find me and figure it out. I said good-bye and got on a plane, hoping something would happen.

I went straight to Los Angeles for a vacation—which I had planned for months—alone. One night I sat alone in my hotel room watching a romantic comedy. When it ended, I burst into tears, sobbing, "Jesus, it's just time. Do it now or never. Either You have somebody for me now or I'm spending the rest of my life alone."

The next day I decided to spend the day at Disneyland drowning my sorrows in churros. When I got back to my car that evening, there was a voice mail on my phone from a number I didn't recognize. My jaw dropped as I heard Skyler's voice telling me he was just calling to say hi and to give him a call back.

Instantly I knew that God had answered my prayer. I knew in my heart that as soon as I called him back, it was all over—I would marry him and never be single again. And then I panicked. I hadn't expected God to answer my prayer so fast! All I could think was, *Am I ready to be married? Am I ready to not be single anymore? I like being single!* In my panic, I didn't call him back.

Skyler called again the next day. I panicked again and watched the call go to voice mail. The day after that, he called a third time, and *again* I watched it go to voice mail. I went to the beach and sat there, crying and trying to figure out what on earth was wrong with me. I wondered if I was feeling scared of marriage because of my childhood. I wondered if I had what it takes to be a good wife. Then through my racing thoughts, I heard that still small voice I had come to know and love.

"Do you trust Me?"

I didn't even need to answer that question. I knew the answer deep in the core of my being. I jumped up, ran to my car to get my phone, and called Skyler back.

The next month, Skyler drove more than nine hours to visit me in Redding. On Saturday, October 18, we went to a pumpkin farm with my sister, her husband, and their kids. While we were there, a stranger asked me, "Are you all going to watch the fireworks tonight?"

"What fireworks?" I asked.

"Tonight's the night they're putting on the Fourth of July fireworks show that got canceled. It's supposed to start pretty soon."

"What?" I couldn't believe it. I immediately told Skyler that fireworks were one of my favorite things and that we had to watch them. When we got downtown, the area was crowded, and it was difficult to find a parking spot. As we hurried to get to the area where the show would happen, we got in a playful argument over who was God's favorite. I told Skyler it was certainly me, and because I was God's favorite, He would hold off the fireworks for me until we found our seats. Sure enough, only when we had made our way through the crowd, found a patch of grass, spread out our blanket, and sat down did the first firework go off. I looked at Skyler with a grin that said, *See?*

As I looked up at the beautiful fireworks, I felt God remind me of the promise made over a year before: "The next time you see the fireworks, you won't be watching them alone." He hadn't said the next Fourth of July. I was instantly overcome with emotion. There I was on a random Saturday in October, watching our "Independence Day" fireworks display with the man I loved. God was faithful to His promise. I was in shock and awe at the kindness of Jesus. As I watched the fireworks, hand in hand with Skyler, I was reminded again that Jesus loves us exactly the way we need to be loved. He doesn't always do things in the way we want them done or exactly when we want them done, but His timing and all His ways are perfect.

When the fireworks were over, I looked at Skyler and said, "What do you want to do now?" I was thinking of getting ice cream.

Skyler responded, "How about spend the rest of my life making you happy?"

By the following Fourth of July, I was watching fireworks with my husband.

Chapter 9 | # HIS JUSTICE

Skyler and I spent our first year of marriage living in San Francisco while I went to acting school. I had done musical theatre growing up and had always loved acting. Before Skyler and I were married, I had begun to feel that familiar restless, "transition is coming" feeling. I discussed it at length with my counselor, trying to figure out what my next step should be. In the end, we landed on this: I was again feeling locked up and like it was time for something new to explore a different side of me. I just wanted to do something for fun! I didn't have any desire to pursue acting seriously. I think there was a part of me that just missed the performance side of being onstage. I am, after all, a bit dramatic.

Of course, that year in San Francisco wasn't just or even mainly about me studying acting, but it was also about Skyler and me laying the foundation of our marriage. We kept traveling for Jesus Culture events and leading worship together, but we spent our days in San Francisco exploring the city and surrounding areas and having fun. When I went to class in the city at night, Skyler walked around taking photos. He had gone to school for graphic design, photography, and art, and he loved capturing artistic shots of the city. In the end, we decided that this year was more about starting our marriage outside of the spotlight of life in a small town and just having fun together. It was time well spent!

After a year, however, these two farm kids were done in the city. We moved back to Redding and bought our first house, which sat on three acres on top of a hill overlooking a little valley. It was a beautiful home that had been built with a lot of loving attention to the details. There was a clawfoot tub in that bathroom that had been salvaged from a farmer's barn. The knobs on the shower door had been found in an antique store in South Carolina. After being inspired by a visit to London, we put up antique-looking wallpaper in some of the rooms.

I loved the breeze that blew through the open windows in the afternoon. I loved the way the sunshine warmed the wide wood floors in the living room. I loved our front porch where we could sit and watch the sun go down. It was happy and peaceful—the perfect setting for God to do some more work in me.

The Layers of Forgiveness

A few months before Skyler and I met, I had an experience that sent me into a whirlwind of anxiety. I went with Banning and Chris to lead worship at a church conference. As soon as we got there, I told Banning that I had a really bad feeling about being there and that something was not right. He encouraged me to just focus on what I was there to do.

The church had sent someone to pick us up from the airport, and the moment I met this person, something just felt off. He ended up being the main contact and driver for me, Chris, and the band. Over the course of our time there, we experienced a couple of strange moments when he seemed upset by us or snapped at us in response to our questions. I chalked it up to his age (he was very young) and decided it was probably an attitude issue that had nothing to do with us. I was really struggling with this uneasy feeling that kept coming over me, and I found it difficult to stay calm and not withdraw.

On the Sunday morning after the conference, Chris and I had been asked to lead worship at the church. Because it was small and couldn't host the entire band, we were doing an acoustic set. Prior to the service, as Chris and I worked through the set list, this person interrupted our conversation and told us we should pick slower, softer songs. He explained that he led worship there most of the time and that because it was early, a lot of people would be tired, and it might be too much for them if we did the bigger songs.

I thought this was a great moment to teach this young worship leader, and I gently tried to explain that worship leaders cannot cater to people's sleepiness. We should instead try to help them engage with some exciting songs and encourage them to engage in praise and worship, despite how they may be feeling.

A short time after we got back home, the church's pastor sent emails to Banning and other leaders at our church that brought multiple accusations against me. The biggest lie was that I had "yelled" at this young man and said, "I'm not here to cater to you." The pastor then emailed me, firing away with angry accusations. He said I had acted like a rock star and treated people very poorly. He never paused to ask any questions but assumed to know everything. I was devastated. I had never had something like this happen before. I had never been accused of the things he accused me of. It made me sick to my stomach to think that anyone would think such horrible things about me. I also felt every justice button inside me being pushed.

From the time I was a little girl, I had a strong sense of right and wrong. In the recurring nightmare about Peter (my mom's second husband), I was always standing between him and my sister, feeling a need to protect her. With Greg, I was the first to call out his behavior for what it was and tried to attack him in self-defense many times. There was an innate cry inside me for justice, a demand that when something is wrong, it should be made right.

Thankfully, when this pastor made these accusations against me, my leaders at Bethel and Banning came to my defense and did not believe a word of it. In their experience, this was something you let roll off your shoulders and move on. But I couldn't get over it so easily. I couldn't stand the thought that such a person existed in the world who not only thought bad things about me but also vocalized those things to others.

When I expressed this to Banning, he gently pointed out that I had a need inside me to please people. At first I balked at this suggestion. But as I took a hard, honest look at myself, I realized the reason this was so devastating was that I hated the idea of someone not liking me. The thought that I couldn't please everyone—as ridiculous as this may sound—was deeply upsetting to me! Banning wanted to help me see that I needed to kill that thing inside me that wanted to please everybody, because it was sure to trip me up later on.

But even after I acknowledged this people-pleasing need in me and asked God to set me free from it, I still felt anger connected to my need for justice. Furious thoughts churned through me whenever I thought about the wrong that had been done to me.

How dare he! How dare this pastor act so carelessly and spew accusations! And did God do anything about it? No! He's still a pastor and still speaking carelessly. This is just like my stepdads. Did God punish them for what they did to me? No, He did not! He doesn't care about the injustices done to me!

When I finally spoke these thoughts out loud, the word that stood out to me was *punish*. I wanted the people who hurt me to be punished, and I wanted God to punish them. Even after forgiving my stepdads and seeing how God had redeemed my story in spite of the wrongs they had done to me, deep down I still had an expectation that if God really loved me, He would execute justice by punishing those who had wronged me. I started to feel angry at God because I didn't see Him punishing them.

Skyler was so caring and gentle with me through all of this. It was such a new and wonderful experience to not have to face these things alone. He was defensive of me, cried with me, and empathized with me, and he also encouraged me toward Jesus. Most of all, he kept loving me through all the ups and downs of my emotions.

At some point in the midst of this struggle, a man named John Arnott spoke at our church. While perusing his book table in the lobby, one of the titles of his books stood out to me: *What Christians Should Know about the Importance of Forgiveness.*

I bought the book and read it in one sitting. Two things impacted me. The first was learning that there are layers to forgiveness. As God peels back one layer and walks you through forgiveness, you get a degree of healing. But down the road, God may use a situation to peel back another layer of pain and reveal something deeper that you may be holding on to, something that requires more forgiveness.

I realized that I had forgiven Peter and Greg, but I hadn't really let them off the hook. Forgiving them had set me free from a lot of pain, but deep down, I still believed they deserved to be punished. I had placed justice into God's hands by forgiving them, but I still expected that His justice would look like punishing them at some point.

As I reviewed the Bible's teachings on forgiveness in Arnott's book, however, I saw that this expectation was wrong. The Bible tells us, "As far as the east is from the west, so far has he removed our transgressions from us" (Psalm 103:12). When Jesus forgives us, He completely removes and forgets about our sin. "He does not treat us as our sins deserve" (Psalm 103:10). We are forgiven, and there is no punishment for us. That is the work of the cross. Jesus took away the curse and the punishment. His version of justice doesn't focus on punishing wrongdoing, but on the restoration of what was lost or damaged by it.

I thought about the pastor who had hurt me. If I was to truly forgive him, it was important that I relinquish my need for him to be punished for what he did. That meant forgiving him, blessing him, and releasing my anger. The entire experience was extremely frustrating, but I could see the kindness of Jesus as He used it to reveal something deeper in me that He wanted to work on. Because He loved me, He allowed the hurt to pull back another layer and expose the old wounds so I could step into greater healing and freedom. I finally saw that it was for my own benefit that He wanted me to forgive and bless the person who had caused me pain. Holding on to the anger only caused darkness and bitterness to grow in my heart, which would ultimately drive a wedge between me and God.

The second thing John Arnott's book clarified for me was

that forgiveness doesn't mean condoning the wrong done to you or the person's poor behavior. I realized I believed that to forgive without demanding punishment was somehow waving a white flag and saying, "You win. It's okay that you treated me that way." That always felt so weak to me. I wanted to fight back to show that the way the person treated me was not okay and that they needed to pay. Yet once I saw the truth, it seemed so obvious that when Jesus forgives our sin, He is not telling us that what we have done is okay. He can only extend forgiveness to us because He paid the terrible price for our sin on the cross, and it's on the basis of that sacrifice that He enables—and requires—us to extend forgiveness to others.

As I began to realize how wrong my thinking had been, I processed it with Jesus. Stepping into a deeper level of forgiveness required me to surrender. Not the kind of surrender that waves a white flag to say I'm too worn down to fight, but rather the brave surrender. The surrender that requires me to lay down my own strength and trust in God's. Our conversation went a little like this:

"God, if I lay down my need for those who hurt me to be punished, it doesn't mean that what they did is okay, right?"

"Right."

"So, just to be clear, we are in agreement that what they did is wrong, correct?"

"Kim, what they did was wrong. I'm sorry you were hurt."

"When I surrender this to You and release those who hurt me, You know for sure that I'm not saying that I agree with them, right?"

"Do you trust Me?"

"I trust You, God, but do I still get to be strong? Does surrendering and letting go mean that I'm weak?"

"Are you relying on your strength or Mine? You are strong when you trust in Me and rely on My strength."

Ugh. And just like that, God broke through another layer of my old need to protect myself through control. It felt so important to me to be strong. My entire childhood I had to be strong for my mom and siblings. I had to be strong to be brave and defend myself. I had to be strong so fear would not cripple me. And it seemed to me that to trust in God, to surrender, to depend on His strength, to forgive those who hurt me, and to not demand punishment meant I could no longer be strong. I hated that!

As I was pondering why this upset me so much, another lie was exposed—the lingering belief that no one can take care of me like I can. Part of me still thought I couldn't really trust God with my heart and emotions.

In the relationships with the abusive stepdads, I tried to be strong, but they had the power and control. I had projected those relationships onto God, thinking that if He had to be the strong one, it meant I had to be the weak one. In my mind, being weak meant I was susceptible to pain and hurt. When I thought about trusting in God's strength to protect me, I couldn't help thinking, *What if He lets me down? What if He doesn't come through for me? What if He doesn't protect me? I don't feel confident that He will do as good a job as I do in taking care of me.*

God gently and lovingly exposed these unhealthy thoughts and beliefs. He showed me that in a healthy relationship, both people can be strong. To trust God and depend on His strength didn't mean I was weak and incapable. When I truly surrendered, I found that it felt so good and freeing to join my strength to His and not be facing everything alone.

In the aftermath of this injustice, my world turned upside

down once again in the most beautiful way by a Father who loved me too much to let me remain in my impaired condition. It was His love that met me right where I was, just as it had many times before, and surrounded me. His love was like a bumper, ensuring that no matter where I ran, I ran right into Him. It brought an assurance that made me feel like I could not fail. No matter how many times I have to sort through these kinds of issues, He's going to make sure I come out on the other side.

So I made a decision. I forgave the pastor who defamed me. I let go of my desire for punishment, and I blessed him. I forgave my stepdads again, but this time I said that I released them and would no longer demand that they pay for what they did. Admittedly, I still needed to remind myself daily that to release them was *not* to condone their actions. I also kept reminding myself that surrendering and trusting God were not acts of weakness but of strength, and that with Him, I not only can be strong, just the way He made me, but I am actually stronger when I trust in His strength and not in my own.

Who Is My Enemy?

Moving to San Francisco for our first year of marriage required me to step down from my role as a worship pastor at Bethel. In the year we were away, God brought in numerous, phenomenal worship leaders, and the team expanded. It was a dream I had longed to see, and it was so beautiful to watch it unfold. I really believe it is essential for me as a worship leader, and as a person who has walked through so much inner healing with Jesus, to raise up other worship leaders who will worship with boldness and passion. It was so encouraging to see the emerging of so many passionate worship leaders.

When we moved back, I had no desire to disrupt what God was building, nor did I want to take away any opportunities for the new leaders. Unfortunately, my transition back to the worship department was awkward. The conversations that probably should have taken place to clarify where I'd fit in with the new roster of worship leaders and what was expected of me now that I was back on the team—but not as a worship pastor—never happened.

As a result, I think the door was left open for people to have lingering questions like, *Does Kim expect us to give her her job back? Does she expect things to run as they did before? If Kim steps back in to lead worship again, am I not going to get to lead as much?* Even the fact that I didn't want to lead worship as often stirred up questions. I had random people at church come up to me and ask if something was wrong and why I wasn't leading anymore.

In the midst of all the confusion, I tried to fight for relationship and make it clear that relationship was most important to me. But as the difficult dynamics continued, I began to give up and withdraw. Also, there were suddenly some stipulations that seemed to be necessary for me to be a part of the team, which made me uncomfortable. It felt as though those stipulations were coming from attempts to assert a degree of power and authority over me, not from a place of leading a family of worshipers. I withdrew further because of this.

Unfortunately, people only saw me retreating and were left to make assumptions about what was going on, leading to misunderstandings about what was happening in my heart. They began to talk, and soon I found myself in another situation where I was being slandered. And this time, the talk didn't just travel through private channels, but it became public on social media. Social media is an amazing tool for connecting with people, but it can also lead to the danger of allowing you to air out your thoughts without processing them, filtering them, and considering the feelings of the other side. In general, I don't think it's a good place to be when emotions are running high.

I must have cried a million tears. I was heartbroken by what people were saying. I wanted to shout my side of the story from the mountaintops and blog it on every social media platform to defend myself and my reputation. The betrayal felt so incredibly painful, especially because it was coming from people close to me. The accusation that had been made was that I had "gone rogue" and was "outside of covering." The allegation implied that I wouldn't allow any leadership to speak into my life and that I wasn't faithfully attending church.

When Skyler and I sat in a room with the people making the accusations, they disclosed that they had gone to other leaders around the world and shared their opinions and frustrations about me, and that these leaders agreed with them. My husband, like the true defender and hero he is, went to battle for me, confronted the people involved, and demanded an apology. After all, it was his wife and her honor being called into question. But at every turn, we were met with resistance, and eventually we realized that we were unlikely to get the apology we were hoping for. We slowly realized that like many churches, there had been small offenses built up over time, but not enough communication to work through it all.

There was a day when the pain of the whole situation became so acute that all I could do was curl up in a ball on the floor of my bedroom and cry out to Jesus.

"Why am I here again?" I asked Him. "Why am I being hurt for no reason? Why is no one making this right?"

"Kim, I love you so much," I heard Jesus reply. "I am creating a foundation inside you that is strong enough to hold up everything I have for you. I will take every opportunity, including this one, to grow you and teach you."

This response didn't sound very appealing. I didn't want to grow anymore. It was so painful! *Couldn't I just be done with growing? Hadn't I grown enough?*

"Why are you running away?" Jesus asked.

Of course, every time Jesus asks a question, I know I'm about to learn something. He undoubtedly knows the answer, but He's wanting me to catch on to a valuable lesson.

Through choking sobs, I responded, "Because I'm hurt. I'm scared and angry, and I don't want to be around those people anymore."

"But who is your enemy?"

"They are!" I shouted.

"Kim, who is your enemy?"

Obviously my first answer wasn't the one He was looking for. Jesus was shining a light into a dark corner of my heart and illuminating something I didn't see.

I realized that I, like so many, had really high expectations of the church and the people in it. Most of the time, the church falls far short of those expectations. I had forgotten that the church is comprised of humans, just like me—humans bound in lies they believe, humans trapped in pain and insecurity, and humans who make bad decisions. When one of them hurt me, I wanted to run away, find another church, or just avoid church altogether. In my pain, I was mistaking them for my enemy instead of remembering that people are not the enemy. I have one enemy, and it is the same one Jesus defeated once and for all when He died on the cross and rose to life the third day.

Tears filled my eyes as I repented for making people my enemy. Realizing the enemy's strategy brought a fresh surge of determination to fight back, but at the right target and in the right way. The enemy wanted to take me out and use relationships close to me to do it. I made the decision in my heart right then and there that I would never allow him to use relationships to try to destroy me again. I determined that one of my core values would be to fight for relationship with the people God put in my life and to cling to my community.

I could tell that Jesus fully backed me in this decision, but He wanted to drive its importance home even further. "Kim, you make yourself more susceptible to the enemy's lies and attacks when you remove yourself from community," He explained. "You become angry, hurt, and bitter and put distance between you and what you believe to be your enemy [the church]. The isolation and disconnection from people just invite the enemy to whisper lies that keep you bound."

His words strengthened my resolve to move forward with a total commitment to keeping my heart clean of all offense, bitterness, and disconnection. Once again, I needed to forgive and let go of any desire for punishment—to protect my connection with Jesus and stay out of confusion and deception that would lead me to fight the wrong battle. I was determined to forgive, love, and to move on.

Of course, as time went on, this commitment to forgive and love was tested repeatedly. Situations arose that stirred up the pain again and put me in a position of having to choose how to engage it. Sometimes a person would come to me and say, "Kim, I heard so-and-so say this-or-that about you. Why would they do that?" On other occasions, the slanderous accusations were completely ignored by those who had heard them, and in a social setting, they felt like a giant elephant in the room.

I met with Banning, who had walked beside me through every step of the entire painful process, to talk about how to handle these scenarios. I told him it felt like I couldn't fully get away from everything that had happened, and I was still having awkward interactions and conversations with people that made me sad and uncomfortable. After expressing how proud he was of me for the choices I had made and how far I had come, he gently pointed out, once again, part of my struggle in these situations seemed to come from that old desire to please people.

When he said it, I felt angry and frustrated—not at him, but at myself. I knew he was right. I could feel that people-pleasing thing in me rearing its ugly head, and I knew it needed to be obliterated from my life. If it didn't, it would control my life and could take me out.

I drove home from meeting with Banning with hot tears streaming down my face and my cheeks flushed with anger. And once again, I felt that familiar voice of God inside me ask, *Do you trust Me?*

By this point in our relationship, I knew that whenever He asked me this question, He was reminding me of the truth of what it means to live a life surrendered to Him. It is a life of constant stretching and growing. In His kindness and goodness, He refuses to leave us in our broken condition and wants to lead us into breakthrough and freedom in every aspect of our lives. In the twelve years since I had fully given my heart to Him, there was never a time when I wasn't growing and learning, stretching and crying, trying and failing, overcoming and achieving. I had long since decided that anyone who says that they are "there" and have "figured it all out" must be crazy and not living in surrender to Jesus. Being grown and stretched was all I knew life with Jesus to be!

It had been two years since we had moved back from San Francisco. This entire process had been long, and I could feel my frustration that it wasn't over yet. At this point, I was leading worship all around the world, recording multiple albums, and teaching—yet I was still a work in progress, and it was clear by the fact that I was circling this mountain again, facing that old foe of people-pleasing, that Jesus was after more growth in my life.

I searched my heart, looking for the answer to His question. Of course I trusted Jesus. Looking back at the previous twelve years, and even at my whole life, I could see His unwavering faithfulness to me. Was there something in my life where I did not trust Him?

In the car, I began to talk out what I was feeling. "I can't stand it that people are saying negative things about me. It means I can't please them, which means I am failing. I want to defend myself. I want to set the record straight. And I didn't see You coming to my defense and setting them straight."

There it was. Jesus wasn't defending me—just like He hadn't defended me with my stepdads. I still didn't fully trust Jesus to be my Defender, because there was still a place in me, even after all the healing, that defaulted to the old lie that He had let me down as a child. I couldn't believe I was going around this mountain *yet again*, but at least by now, I knew exactly what needed to be done, and I wasted no time doing it. I forgave my stepdads once more. I released them and blessed them. And I again forgave the people who had slandered me.

I decided that if I was truly surrendered to Jesus, I could trust Him with my reputation. If He was my Defender, then I didn't need to defend myself. I also decided that because I was living a life surrendered to Jesus and living in community with mothers, fathers, sisters, and brothers around me, the fruit of my life would speak for itself. The fruit of a life surrendered to Jesus tells an even greater story than someone just trying to defend themselves.

Chapter 10

THE KNOCK-DOWN-DRAG-OUT WITH FEAR

In December 2012, Skyler and I decided that, while we would remain committed to Jesus Culture, it was time to leave Redding. By this point, Jesus Culture had become a movement with a flourishing record label. Banning, Chris, and I were still working together, just as smoothly as we had for the last twelve years. Because we did conferences and events around the world and recorded music, realistically, Skyler and I could live anywhere and meet up with our team wherever we were doing ministry. We began to pray about where to go and what God would have us do.

A month after this decision, I got a phone call from Banning. He had always wanted to plant a church, but he didn't want to do it without being sent out and blessed by our pastors and church leadership at Bethel. He told me he met with the senior leader, Bill Johnson, who told him it was time and that he wanted to send us out to plant a church. I was stunned. My heart leaped at the idea that I would get to leave Redding with my Jesus Culture community and would get to start a church together! I felt in awe once again at the goodness of God. He was leading Skyler and me out, but we wouldn't be going alone.

Not alone, indeed. Only a few days after that phone call, I found out I was pregnant with our first child. There aren't enough words to describe the whirlwind of emotions I felt. I was scared of becoming a mother, excited to be starting our family, and anxious about uprooting and moving in the middle of it all. Skyler and I spent a lot of time praying and thinking it over and ultimately made the tough decision to stay behind in Redding a little longer, until after our baby was born. It felt overwhelming to move and settle into a new city while pregnant. We had no idea what to expect with a pregnancy, let alone a new church plant, and didn't want to create any added stress in our growing family.

By February, the Bethel leaders publicly announced that Jesus Culture was being sent out to plant a church. In June, our entire team moved to Sacramento, California, and began to hold meetings with a group of about a hundred people who would form the core of the church. We wanted our internal world to be able to sustain the external world, so we began building our community culture with this group and setting up a foundational structure to sustain the church when we opened the doors to the public.

Throughout my pregnancy, Skyler and I made the three-hour drive back and forth between Redding and Sacramento to be part of the core team meetings. In September, I gave birth to a little boy, whom we named Wyatt. I had Wyatt at my midwife's house and had to work very hard to birth my baby boy. My entire face was swollen from pushing so hard for so long, and my eyes were nothing more than little slits on my face. As Skyler passed him to me, I just saw what looked to be a blurry baby with two heads coming at me.

"What's wrong with his head?" I shouted.

"Don't worry, sweetie," my midwife said. "He was just really squished in there, and it'll go back to normal in no time."

She was right. Within a few hours, Wyatt's head was fine, and I found myself lost in a swirl of exhaustion, terror, joy, and out-of-my-mind love.

A few weeks later, we put our house on the market and headed to Sacramento. Despite our efforts to lower the stress around this transition, it was still quite challenging because of how much I had on my plate. Of course, I was navigating the emotional roller coaster of learning to be a mom. I worried about every tiny thing with the baby and if I was "doing it right." I spent countless hours crying, either because he was just so beautiful or because I was just so stressed.

But even though I had just had a baby, we didn't slow down! We took Wyatt to Russia when he was four months old. By the time he turned one, he had been in thirteen different countries and nineteen different states. In addition to traveling, leading worship, and working on various Jesus Culture albums, I was now president of Jesus Culture Music, our label, which was quite a lot of work. I loved running the business side of Jesus Culture, felt like I was learning a lot, and enjoyed working with numbers again—but adding that to my life made for a *very* full plate.

Hitting the Wall

When Wyatt was six months old, I found out to my shock that I was pregnant again. I took a couple of days to catch my breath and wrap my head around caring for a baby and being pregnant at the same time. Then I just put my head down and kept going. I was so overwhelmed by trying to figure out how to be a good mom in the midst of my crazy life, and I didn't even want to consider what on earth I would do with two children!

Getting settled in Sacramento had been proving to be more difficult than we had anticipated. Thinking it wouldn't take long for our house in Redding to sell, we signed a short-term lease on a rental when we first moved. However, the house didn't sell before our lease ended, and we had to find another place to live. We ended up moving twice more before we finally accepted that we needed to settle into a longer-term rental.

In the midst of all that, we suffered another setback in September 2014. Skyler, Wyatt, and I were on an extended trip to New Zealand when we received word from Skyler's parents that they had stopped at our house in Redding to stay for a night, only to find that it had flooded. The next day Skyler got on the phone with our insurance company to discuss our flood coverage and learned that the flooding had caused an estimated thirty thousand dollars' worth of damage.

While he was on the phone, I received a panicked call from our realtor. She had been leading a team of cleaners over to our house to begin the process of cleaning up all the damage, only to come upon a roadblock. Apparently a huge forest fire was raging out of control and heading straight toward our house. Our neighborhood had already been evacuated, and there was no way she could get out there.

I frantically relayed the information to Skyler, who began asking our insurance agent if we also had coverage for fire damage! Being all the way across the Pacific Ocean, the only thing we could do was pray.

The next morning we got a phone call. Winds had suddenly appeared and pushed the fire back into an area that had previously been burned and was already evacuated, so no one was harmed. It was no longer a threat to any homes, and the firefighters were confident they could get it contained. Jesus had heard our prayers!

Two days later Skyler went on an overnight ocean fishing trip with a local pastor. I stayed at the hotel with Wyatt, who had been fighting a fever. As a new mom (and one who was seven months pregnant!), I was so nervous and trying everything I could to help him feel better. The morning after Skyler left, I woke up to find Wyatt with a fever of 102 degrees. When I picked him up, he lay there limply, staring and unresponsive. Absolute panic kicked in. I called the pastor's wife and asked her to take me to the hospital. They took us in right away and started giving Wyatt fluids and checking him out. I stood there, feeling helpless, scared, and convinced I must be a horrible mother to have a sick baby in a foreign country.

This probably wouldn't have even happened if you had stayed at home with your baby like other moms do. He probably caught something while he was on the airplane. You're a bad mom. And you're pregnant. Probably gonna be a bad mom to that kid too.

To make matters worse, I couldn't reach Skyler. Talk about stress.

At last the doctor informed me that Wyatt had an infection and prescribed some antibiotics. Thankfully he started perking up by the time we made it out of the hospital. I, however, was nearing the end of myself.

The truth was that my busyness had been my way of dealing with a fear that had been growing in me before and throughout this second pregnancy. Only a few weeks before I found out I was pregnant, a close friend lost her baby due to anencephaly. As I grieved with her and mourned the loss of her precious baby girl, the fear that something would go wrong with my child took root in my heart.

I started having nightmares in which I would find myself standing over Wyatt's crib, gripping his head with both hands and screaming. After finding out I was pregnant, the nightmares got worse. When I had an ultrasound done at five months, I told the technician I didn't want to know the gender—I only wanted to know if my baby was alive and had a head that was completely intact. She looked at me in confusion and assured me my baby was totally healthy.

Just two months before the ultrasound, when I was three months pregnant, I had gone on tour for my solo record *Still Believe*. One of our dates was in New York City, and we had sold out a theater in Times Square. I was so excited! But the morning of the concert, I woke up with excruciating pain and cramps. I could barely walk or move because the pain was so intense. Skyler got me to a hotel room so I could try to sleep it off, but I couldn't sleep. I was certain I was experiencing a miscarriage and was losing the baby.

Finally Skyler took me to the emergency room. They got me in right away and told me that an ultrasound technician was on the way to check on the baby. I changed into a hospital gown, got into the hospital bed, grabbed Skyler's hand, and wept. My body was trembling with fear that my baby was dead. I was trying to prepare myself for the worst news, but I couldn't hold myself together. After what felt like an eternity, the technician arrived and began the ultrasound. I held my breath.

"There's your little bean, and there is a perfect heartbeat!" he said.

I let out my breath and sobbed.

He continued. "Your baby is totally healthy, and there are no signs of a miscarriage."

Skyler and I cried tears of relief. They found I had an infection that was causing the pain and cramping, gave me a prescription, and sent me on my way. On the drive back to the venue, Skyler said it was only an hour until showtime and everyone was wondering if we should cancel. It seemed like the best idea, considering I could barely walk and was still in a tremendous amount of pain. But after hearing that my baby was okay, I was furious—at fear for convincing me I had lost my baby, at the enemy for filling my mind with lies, and at myself for listening to those lies and allowing terror to overwhelm me.

"I'm going to make the enemy pay," I told Skyler. "I am getting on that stage tonight. We are going to worship, and we are going to see people get set free tonight."

I understood that the enemy would love nothing more than to stop me from leading people into God's presence and getting set free and healed, and I wasn't about to let that happen. Skyler let the team know I was still going on. Once I arrived at the venue, I got dressed, warmed up, and went onto that stage. Though the physical pain was still intense, I pressed through it, and we had an incredible night of worship.

When the evening came to an end, I sat in my dressing room thinking about the day's events. I realized I needed to forgive myself for giving in to the fear. But I also realized that while it was a good choice to press through and keep worshiping, a day of reckoning was coming. I could not outrun the things God was wanting to address inside me. Fear and anxiety kept launching attacks, and I knew He wanted to set me free from that. I was still struggling to trust God—not just with myself, but also with my baby.

That day of reckoning came soon after we returned from New Zealand. I had finally reached a point in my pregnancy where I *had* to slow down and begin to prepare for baby number two. When I did, it felt as though I had run smack into a wall. I had been running hard and refusing to rest, in part because there were some things inside me that I didn't want to confront. Now, these things emerged in the quiet and finally got my attention. I felt God gently pulling on my heart and drawing me to Him. It was time to have an honest conversation about the fear and my struggle to trust Him.

"Jesus, I'm scared to trust You with my babies," I admitted. "I'm scared that You will let me down. I'm scared that You aren't capable of taking care of them as well as me. I'm also scared that You won't take care of them the way I want You to."

Ugh. Those last words hit me like a slap in the face. My need for control had surfaced once again. Pregnancy was a situation I couldn't fully control. I was eating healthy, taking my vitamins, and doing everything I could to protect and nurture this human growing inside me, but ultimately, I could not control whether this baby grew the way it should. I couldn't control how the birth would go or whether the baby would live or die. I hated feeling out of control! In my desperation, I had grasped for anything that would give me a sense of control—in this case, I had attempted to build a wall of busyness between myself, my baby, and Jesus.

I could feel the tender love of my Father begin to pour out on me. It was like a warm, gentle breeze that surrounded me, blowing away the dust that had settled over truths I knew but had been refusing to remember. Jesus reminded me of how much He loved me, that I belonged to Him, and that He created me. He reminded me of the time He had shown me how He created me—how He ripped a chunk from His own heart and brought me back to that place in His heart where only I fit.

As I remembered the love of my Father and Creator, I understood that this was the same love He had for my babies. He created them and chose them, just like He chose me. He loved them with the same unrelenting love with which He loved me. The Bible says in 1 John 4:18 that "perfect love drives out fear." My need for control was totally rooted in fear—no discussion needed. As God stirred up His love inside me, it began to push fear out, enabling me once again to surrender my need for control to the One who holds my life and future. I saw myself putting my babies in God's outstretched arms, and I felt His peace that goes beyond my understanding resting on my mind and heart.

The Final Battles

Skyler and I had decided we wanted to have our second birth in Redding with the same midwife we had used with Wyatt. Our house in Redding had finally sold, but we wouldn't close until all the renovations from the flooding had been repaired. The closing date was set for December 22, 2014, and our baby was due on Christmas Day. Some friends had a rental in Redding that they made available for us to use, and on the first of December, we signed the papers on our house and hunkered down to await the arrival of our baby.

Just a few days after arriving in Redding, we were driving to a checkup when we got a phone call from Banning. Alyssa Quilala, wife of Chris Quilala, was eight months pregnant, and they had just received the devastating news that their baby did not have a heartbeat. I hung up the phone, leaned back in the passenger seat, and began to pray out loud for the peace of God and for their baby boy to come back to life. Suddenly my praying turned into frantic, incoherent screams, and I began to hyperventilate as I was swallowed whole by a massive, dark wave of fear. I could feel myself sinking into an abyss of terror. Just one thought surged through my mind like a runaway train: *What if my baby dies?*

Skyler pulled the car over, grabbed me, and tried to get me to breathe and snap out of it. His voice sounded far away, but I clung to it like a drowning victim to a lifesaver. As he slowly reeled me back to reality, I started to catch my breath, and tears began to pour from my eyes.

"My baby! What if my baby is dead?" My words were tumbling out of my mouth. "Do you think my baby is dead?"

"It's okay, hon. The baby is okay," Skyler assured me. "Just breathe. Come on. Deep breaths."

I wanted to believe him, but it was a struggle. Only when I arrived at my checkup and heard the baby's heartbeat on the Doppler did I finally settle down.

We went to the memorial service for Chris and Alyssa's baby. I wanted to support my friends, but my body was wracked with fear. When they started a video slideshow with pictures of their beautiful boy, my entire body began to shake violently. I was so overcome with fear. Skyler put both arms around me and tried as hard as he could to hold me still. I was totally surrendered to the fear that encompassed me. I couldn't even fathom trusting God. I felt betrayed by Him because He hadn't preserved this tiny baby's life.

My friend who had lost her child to anencephaly heard about the Quilalas' stillbirth and called to check on me. Earlier that year, I had opened up to her about the fear I experienced after the death of her daughter and finding out I was pregnant. She asked if she could set up an online counseling appointment with a man who had been counseling her. I agreed to do it, but I knew I needed to do some work even to get myself to a place where I could confront my fear with a counselor.

I recognized that one of the issues contributing to my battle with fear was that I had become wrapped up in trying to find answers to the question that the losses of my friends' babies naturally provoked: "Why?" Unfortunately, that question, so often asked in the face of suffering, death, and loss, is one for which we rarely get any kind of satisfactory answer, and if we get hung up on it, we can damage our faith and trust in God.

Bill Johnson once preached a sermon—one I listened to many times—that addressed the reality we live in and the mysteries we wrestle with. We understand that God is powerful—He can heal, set us free, and perform miracles. Yet these are not always the outcomes we get, at least in the way or timing we expect. Why do some people get a miracle and some do not? As Christians, we live in that place of tension where things don't always make sense. The big question is what we will do while living in that tension. Do we choose to trust and worship God, regardless of the outcome? Or do we shake our fist at Him, allow our hearts to become offended, and put distance between us and Him?

As they had many times before, these thoughts strolled down the hallway of my mind. But I finally decided that once again I would choose God. I knew He was my only hope for freedom from the torment of fear. I knew I must choose Him above my demand for answers. Once I got my heart to that place, I was ready to talk to the counselor.

Over Skype I explained to the counselor the fear I had been living in all year and my struggle to trust God completely. I had a big job ahead of me—birthing a baby—and I couldn't go into it with all this fear!

The counselor agreed and said the most important thing was to get my heart connected to the heart of God again. He asked me to close my eyes and recall the most recent time I felt the most connected to Jesus.

I closed my eyes and allowed my mind to drift and remember. Interestingly, the moment that came to mind was Wyatt's birth. Wyatt was born face up, and I had to push for four hours to deliver him because his head was resting on his shoulder, which caused him to be stuck. Yet the whole time, I felt incredible peace. Every time I closed my eyes, I could see Jesus standing over me with His arms stretched out, holding back a dark cloud of fear. It was almost as if He created a circle of protection around me. Even though he was stuck, Wyatt's heartbeat never once faltered. He was just as calm as I was and undoubtedly felt that peace.

As I remembered this moment, tears began to flow, and I felt that same peace coming over me again. I saw Jesus standing over me and pulling back the dark cloud of fear, and I felt myself once again settling into that bubble of protection.

The counselor asked, "Is there something you would like to ask Jesus?"

In this moment of calm and peace, I felt the courage to ask the question at the forefront of my mind. To my surprise, it wasn't quite what I thought it would be.

"Do You love my baby?"

I suddenly realized that the fear of my baby dying was rooted in a lie that God did not love my baby. How could I trust Him with my baby if He didn't even care about my baby? *Where did that lie come from?* I wondered. I thought about it and decided it must have come from the belief that I was unprotected and unloved by God as a child. Of course, at this point in my life, I knew it was not true. But when faced with a situation like this, my brain and emotions still behaved as though this were true. God had given me the truth, but it was still a battle for me to get that truth to transform my behaviors and reactions.

I saw a picture of Jesus walking toward me with the biggest grin on His face. His eyes were completely lit up with joy. He reached out His hand, put it on my heart, and said, "Can you feel that? Can you feel the joy? This baby is pure joy and happiness. I am so excited about this baby!"

I began to laugh as I felt His joy. It was overwhelming. I could feel Jesus' excitement over this child in my womb and the joy inside my belly. My baby was moving around, as if to say, *Yes! I am full of joy!*

I knew there was still pain in there and work to be done, but I felt reconnected to Jesus and ready to have my baby. On the morning of December 22, we welcomed another boy into the world. We named him Bear and decided he needed a name that expressed the gift of joy he is. One of his middle names is Kaemon—an old Japanese Samurai name that means "joyful."

December 22 was also the day that we closed on our house

in Redding. It felt like the end of one chapter and the beginning of a new chapter, all in one day.

Sleepless Nights and a Sudden Loss

The next two years proved to be the hardest I had endured in a long, long time. It was very challenging to have two babies only fourteen months apart. There were many times I felt that having twins would have been easier! Just as one would exit a stage, the other would be entering it.

Wyatt looks just like Skyler, but his personality is much like his mama's. He loves to be the center of attention and is always trying to bring out a laugh in everybody. He has a very strong will and a strong need not just to be told something but to really understand it. Bear looks exactly like me but has a temperament more like Skyler. He lives in his own little world most of the time and is content to be alone. He too has a very strong personality! They are both adventurous and curious, which was evident in the early days.

In those two years, I worked partly from home and partly at the Jesus Culture offices. I remember many times when I'd be sitting at home breastfeeding Bear while on a conference call, and a babysitter was playing with Wyatt in another room. Meetings were scheduled around naps, and when I came into the offices, it was pretty normal for the staff to see me with a baby in tow.

As a newborn, Bear had severe reflux issues that caused him to be fussy and upset most of the time. It was so hard to spend so much time tediously trying to get a newborn to eat and calm down while trying to give attention to my one-year-old.

One day when Bear was still only a few months old, I was looking through some photos of the Christmas after Bear was born. He was only three days old, and suddenly as I looked at Wyatt, a sad truth struck me. He was still only a baby! In most of the pictures, Wyatt was wearing a diaper, had a pacifier in his mouth, was drinking out of a bottle, could only say a few words, had hardly any hair on his head, and was unstable on his feet.

I burst into heavy sobs as I realized that the moment Bear was born, I didn't see Wyatt as the baby anymore. He looked so big compared to Bear! I needed him to be older more quickly now that I had another baby, and without even thinking about it, I had expected a lot more from him. I felt horrible. Grief and shame were slapping me across the face.

That night when I tucked Wyatt into bed, I said to him, "Wyatt, I am so sorry if I wasn't there for you the way you needed me to be when Bear was born. I'm sorry that I expected more from you than what you were ready to give. Will you forgive me?"

Wyatt looked at me with quizzical eyes. I'm sure he was too young to understand everything I was saying, but it didn't matter. I knew his little spirit could hear me and understand, just as I had understood things as a little girl. It was important. A big grin flashed across his little face, and he said, "I yuv you, Mama." My heart melted.

The other bane of my existence in these years was the total annihilation of good sleep. Neither Wyatt nor Bear were good sleepers. Perhaps it was that they were always in a different time zone, in a different bed, in a different room, and in a different environment. I didn't sleep through the night *once* during the first three years after Wyatt was born. I didn't understand at the time how badly this lack of sleep was affecting me mentally, but I would soon find out.

Skyler had dreamed of opening a board shop, so we decided to make it happen. We opened a snowboard and skateboard shop in Folsom, California. I took on all the accounting for the store while continuing to run Jesus Culture's record label, record albums, travel, and help with the church plant. I was still running full steam ahead—on fumes.

Toward the end of April 2015, our whole family went on tour with Jesus Culture to Brazil. While we were there, I got a phone call from my mom.

Without preamble, she said, "Kim, the doctor has put George in hospice."

George had been diagnosed with Parkinson's disease about eleven years before and had undergone multiple brain surgeries and various treatments. I couldn't fully understand Parkinson's disease or how serious it was or wasn't. There were many times when he seemed to be getting better, but also scary periods when his health seemed to rapidly decline. However, his sense of humor remained intact. He had started to develop dementia because of the disease and had joked that I now had two dads with brain damage. Sometimes laughing was the only thing that got us through hard moments when we didn't know what else to say, think, or do.

I couldn't understand my emotions with George. By this point, we had become good friends, and I had grown to really love him and appreciate him, but I hadn't yet been able to recognize all the important ways he had impacted me, my family, and my faith. I still held him at a distance at times. As his health grew worse and he began to lose his ability to speak, I found myself in conversations with him that made me uncomfortable.

"Kim?"

"Yes, George?"

"You know I love you, right? We've had a good relationship, you and I, right?"

"Yes, George. Of course."

I wasn't entirely sure why he was asking these questions, but it hinted that part of me was still afraid to fully open my heart to George and express my love for him—and he knew it. There was still some of that little girl in there who felt afraid of being hurt and rejected. And I responded to this hint as I do with things I don't really want to face: I got busy. I didn't want to think about George leaving us for heaven or have a vulnerable conversation with him that required me to open my heart wider.

So when my mom told me George had gone into hospice, I found myself speechless. For starters, I wasn't even sure what hospice was or what it meant. She went on to explain that George was nearing the end of his life and that I should come to say good-bye. I took a deep breath, sucked in every painful and helpless emotion that wanted to come raging out of me at that moment, and began to work on a plan to get to Oregon.

We were at the tail end of the Brazil tour, so we made it home only a short time later. The day after we landed in California, Skyler and I loaded the kids onto another plane, flew to Oregon, dropped the kids off at my mom's house, and went straight to the hospice house to see George.

When I walked in, I barely recognized him. His body had been ravaged by the disease, and he looked frail and small lying in the bed. George had always been a handsome man. (Many women thought he looked a lot like George Clooney—he loved that!)

I walked to his bedside, sat down, and managed to squeak

out his name. George slightly opened his eyes for a moment, and I knew he was listening and had recognized me. I let out that breath I had been holding in since the phone call in Brazil, and with it came a flood of tears and emotions. It was as though my heart had burst open and allowed that vulnerable little girl who had been abused and hurt by men and who desperately wanted to be loved and protected to finally admit she had found what she was looking for with George.

"George, thank you for rescuing us!" I sobbed. "I'm so sorry I couldn't say it until now. But I'm so thankful for you. Thank you for loving me even when I rejected you!"

He had been a dad, more than I had wanted to admit or allow myself to see. He had been unrelenting in loving me, even when I refused to love him back. I told him he was the reason I was a Christian, and that I didn't even want to imagine what my life would have been like had he not come along. I thanked him for loving my mom and adopting my baby brother. I asked his forgiveness for not being able to open up my heart until now.

Suddenly George's eyes opened, and he said, "Kim, sing that song for me—the one I love!"

I knew he was referring to "Healing Oil," a simple chorus on my solo record *Still Believe*. That album was all about healing, and I had written many of the songs with George in mind. It was one of his favorite albums, and he listened to it all the time.

Through my tears and sobs, I began singing the song the best I could. I watched as George's mouth twitched like he was trying to sing along, and he managed to slightly lift his arm, like he was trying to stretch it out in worship. George never stopped worshiping and loving Jesus. He never stopped asking Jesus to heal him and never stopped believing it could happen.

George went to live with Jesus on May 16, the day after my sixth wedding anniversary.

A New Kind of Grief

Though I felt joy that George was no longer in pain, I cried for days and months after his death. It seemed now that I had allowed the doors of my heart to fling open and vulnerability to spill out, I couldn't get the doors shut again. Memories flooded my mind—moments with George that were so precious and that I had taken for granted. I was a mess. I was still sleep-deprived. I was stressed from all the things I had going on in my life and couldn't seem to get control over.

Guilt and shame came in. *I'm a leader,* I thought. *I shouldn't be such a mess!* I was trying to hold everything together and convince everyone I was okay. I was trying to be wise and help my husband run his shop and support his dream. I was trying to be a perfect mom for my boys, always comparing myself to other moms and feeling like I was coming up short. In my mind, I couldn't appear weak, out of control, or messy. But when I stepped onstage to lead worship and sing certain lyrics, I was thinking, *Do I really believe this? Do I really think God is a "God of miracles"? After all, George never got his miracle.* I could feel myself longing to wrestle through my faith—and my doubts—but would instantly shut it down. I could feel the familiar anger I had as a teen rearing its ugly face again, taunting me with blaming God. How could I, a worship leader and someone whom people looked up to, waver in my belief?

In the darkest moments, when the sleep deprivation overtook

me, I had dark thoughts of wanting to hurt myself and make the pain stop. I had heard that voice before—the voice that says to end it all. It's funny—I think a lot of people who have never heard that voice would imagine it to be dark, scary, and angry. But it is actually a calm and soothing voice, which just adds to the evil deceit. After those thoughts came, I recognized how rash they were, but then I'd beat myself up for having such bad thoughts.

My mom came for a visit a few months after George passed away. One morning I came downstairs and walked into the kitchen, mumbling things to myself. I was deliriously tired and angry about it. My mom gently said, "Kim, I think you might have postpartum depression."

I laughed out loud. "Oh my word, Mom! Believe me, I do *not* miss being pregnant!"

"Hon, I don't think postpartum depression means what you think it means," she said.

I went back upstairs and lay down on my bed. I picked up my phone and wondered if my mom was right. I thought that postpartum depression was when women loved being pregnant so much that they missed it after the baby was born. At the moment, being pregnant sounded like the absolute worst thing that could happen to me, so I didn't believe I had depression. Then I Googled "postpartum depression." My mouth dropped open as I read the definition and symptoms, which perfectly described me. I jumped up, ran downstairs in tears, and shouted, "I have postpartum depression!"

I was so angry at myself. *How could I let this happen?* I didn't want to be put on medications, so I did a lot of research, looking for natural options to help me. I researched different vitamins and supplements and began to exercise and watch my diet. I also started to see a counselor on a regular basis. I was trying so hard to make everything perfect and clean up the mess I found myself in.

Letting Him into the Mess

Then Jesus came knocking. One day, as I sat alone while my babies napped, I felt Jesus at the door of my heart, wanting to come in. It was one of those moments when it suddenly feels like the whole atmosphere changes in the room because Jesus has just showed up and you weren't expecting it at all. You are both shocked and excited. I was taken off guard but also felt a sense of relief that maybe He was there to help me out of my present circumstances. However, my immediate reaction was to scramble around, trying to clean up the messy house of my heart. *I can't let the God of the universe come into this mess!* I thought frantically. *I need to clean it up and make everything perfect for Him.*

But He just kept knocking and asking me to please let Him in, and finally I surrendered. I could not fight it anymore. I fully expected Him to walk into my heart, chastise me for what a mess it was, and punish me for allowing the negative things to come in. I was certain He would express His great disappointment with me.

Instead Jesus came in and wrapped His arms around me. The mess didn't even faze Him. He didn't punish me or yell at me. He just held me, right there in all the mess.

"We are going to get through this," He told me. "But we are going to do it together, hand in hand. It's going to be one step at a time. We aren't in a rush. Right now I just want to sit here with you and tell you how much I love you."

His love was relentless! He did not slow down or stop when I refused to open the door. He did not quit moving toward me when I expressed my anger and frustration. He did not punish me when I needed to wrestle through my faith. Jesus actually wanted to be in the mess and the process with me. Most importantly, He was on my side. He was for me and not against me. It was His great love and kindness that moved me toward healing and wholeness, wanting me to be the best version of myself.

I let Him into the mess, and there I felt something familiar. I could feel the pulling and the prompting of Holy Spirit, asking my heart to surrender. I suddenly felt what I can only describe as angry exasperation.

Really? Again? You want me to surrender again? I am so tired of surrendering. Why am I even here, going around this mountain again? What haven't I surrendered to You? Look at me! I have nothing left to give! I surrender everything to You—and You stand in front of me, demanding more?

When I had tried to end my life and found myself saved by Jesus, I had surrendered my life to Him. When I was going through inner healing and facing my anger and pain toward the men who had hurt me, I had surrendered it all to Jesus. When I was called to Africa and terrified, I had surrendered my fear to Jesus. When I knew it was time to step out and move, I had trusted Jesus. When I was slandered and accused, I had surrendered my pain to Jesus and my need for punishment. When I was terrified that Jesus would let my babies die, I had surrendered them to Him. I felt as if my whole life could be summed up into that one word: *surrender.*

Then I heard these simple words: "Am I not worthy?"

Tears spilled out of me as my mind pulled the answer to that question to the forefront. I remembered how God built everything I needed to survive my childhood inside me. He sent George and saved my life. He saved me when I had tried to end my life. He brought me the right people to help lead me into healing and deliverance. Moment after moment, memory after memory—all reminded me that *yes*, He is worthy. So I mustered all my courage and surrendered again. I lay down my strength, ambition, and need for control and yielded my heart to Him once more. I brought my sacrifice of praise—the worship that felt like it was costing me my very life in that moment.

What happened next followed the pattern I had experienced every time I surrendered to Jesus: He began to expose lies I'd been believing and lead me into freedom. There were two lies I had been believing about who I was, particularly as a mother. I had believed that because I was such a mess and had walked through so much in my life, I was not capable of being a good mom. I thought the best thing for my boys was for me to put some distance between myself and them. I would love them and take care of them, but it was as if I was always running a little ahead of them and telling them to keep following me. It completely broke my heart to realize I was putting space between my heart and theirs.

I had also been believing the lie that I couldn't be fulfilled just being a mother—that I was fulfilled with either a job or kids, and it couldn't be both. Jesus revealed the truth that He had chosen me—overachieving, world-traveling, worship-leading, heart-exploding, drama-loving me—to be their mama. He gave those boys to me and wanted me to raise them. He showed the capacity of my heart and how I can be completely fulfilled being a mother and fulfilled having a job. It's okay for me to choose both of those things.

But Jesus did have something very important to add to that. "Don't forget to honor their sacrifice," He told me.

My children have sacrificed a lot. They haven't had routines and structured stability like many other children do. They are always in a different time zone, a different state, a different hotel, and the like. They've had to share their mama with a stage and a lot of people. I felt Jesus reminding me to honor them for what it has cost and will cost them.

I knew this meant there would be seasons when I need to pay attention to their signals, and that when they need a break from all the adventuring, it's time to stop. And at the end of 2015, they made it clear they were ready to take a break. They were suddenly irritable and fussy nonstop. They threw a fit about every tiny thing. Every time we left our rental house, they begged for their toys and their beds. It was obvious the need for a break had arrived.

Chapter 11 | LOVE DRIVES OUT FEAR

I told God that if we were going to take a break from traveling so much and stay home, we needed a true home. Skyler and I were about to lose our minds in the Sacramento suburbs. God came through for us, and on May 15, 2016 (our seventh wedding anniversary), we became the owners of a small farmhouse with five beautifully landscaped acres about an hour outside of Sacramento. We soon added chickens, goats, and one black sheep my boys affectionately named Donut. We then spent a year resting, allowing our boys to get settled into a routine and soaking up the peace that filled our home.

That first summer in our new place, we spent countless nights on our back deck eating dinner and watching the boys play. Skyler and I felt so content—like we could finally catch our breath and reflect on the wild, rewarding, and often painful season that finally seemed to be coming to a close. Yet as we sat there chatting about our day and discussing the future, a nagging feeling kept nipping at the back of our minds. We both felt it. It was the feeling that someone was missing in our family.

I brought it up one night. Skyler admitted to the same feeling, but we were quick to dismiss it. We both agreed we didn't want to deal with pregnant Kim or Kim-with-a-newborn ever again! But that feeling would not leave me alone. It was similar to the feeling you get when you leave the house in a hurry and feel like you forgot something. Your mind is scrambling down a list trying to figure out what you forgot, and you can't seem to land on anything!

One day I was out driving somewhere, the boys preoccupied with a movie in the back of our minivan, when my mind began to drift. I had that familiar sense that God wanted to discuss something with me. A question floated into my mind.

"What are you afraid of?"

My eyes started to brim with tears. I was thinking back to the season I had finally emerged from—the difficulty of having two babies in fourteen months, the heaviness of postpartum depression, the trauma of childbirth, the trauma of close friends losing babies, the anxiety of moving multiple times, the challenge of planting a church, the stress of having multiple jobs, and the pain of losing George. The idea of getting pregnant again and having another baby scared the living daylights out of me. What if I got depression again? What if the birth was traumatic? What if my baby died? What if my baby lived but was a horrible sleeper and I became completely sleep-deprived again?

Then I remembered my new eyes—the eyes God had given me so many years ago when He healed me and brought total integration to all the fractured pieces of my heart. Those new eyes had provided a new lens with which to view my life. When I looked back at my life, I saw a story that had been redeemed. God totally changed my perspective of my life and helped me to see Him there with me throughout my whole life.

I picked up that lens and looked again at the season that was slowly fading behind me. I had gone around the mountain again, uncertain I could fully trust God. I had been required to surrender again—but just as He had always done, God met me in the place of wild, uncertain abandon. I saw how I had wanted to give up many times and disqualify myself, but God was there, fighting with me and for me. I could see myself grabbing hold of His strength as He stood in the mess with me. Together we had faced head-on the dragon named Fear and defeated it.

I smiled as I realized that fear no longer had a grip on me! My heart was bursting as I noticed that every time I took a moment to give my attention to Jesus, lift my face, and set my eyes on Him, I saw that He already had His eyes on me. It's a steadfast gaze that guides and leads me. I could see I was no longer held hostage by the doubts and the questions. My heart began to surge to life, and excitement flowed through me as I saw the story of the last season rewritten by the One who loves me. And as I drove along reflecting on all this, I decided there was no reason to fear anymore.

In early October, I found out I was pregnant. On June 9, 2017, we welcomed a sweet, healthy baby girl, whom we named Maisie. It felt like a kiss from heaven to have a little girl after years of living in a world of men, both with the band and at home.

For Maisie's delivery, I had to have a scheduled cesarean section. Through some strange scheduling errors, the doctor kept moving the date for the surgery. This stressed me, because one thing I was really concerned about with a C-section was whether the baby was actually ready to come out when scheduled. It felt strange understanding what the Bible says about our lives—that every day is ordained and known by God—and picking a random day with the doctor for my baby to be born!

Eventually they landed on June 9 at 7 a.m. Well, Miss Maisie's entire family is full of strong personalities who don't like to be told what to do, and she is no exception! I went into labor the night before, arrived at the hospital dilated eight centimeters, and Maisie took her first breath at 6:59 a.m.!

Maisie means "pearl," and she is most certainly my precious reward after a long and arduous battle. Having her is like having a built-in best friend! She is intuitive with me, like a friend, noticing the changes in my emotion or countenance. She is by far my calmest and most peaceful, easy baby. The best part of all? She sleeps thirteen hours a night!

And the sweetest relationship is the one she has with her brothers. They adore her—both of them are completely smitten! They are so tender with her and eager to dote on her, smothering her with hugs and kisses. One day while eating lunch, Wyatt was staring at his baby sister with the most affectionate smile and loving eyes. He turned and looked at me and said, "Mama, I love Maisie *so* much." I'm so thankful I leaped out in surrender to Jesus once again, trusting Him with another baby.

When We Surrender, We Can't Mess Up the Story

I have come to understand the sovereignty of God. There are no surprises to Him and nothing hidden from Him. I have never witnessed Him step down from heaven to control a person here on earth. The most beautiful gift He gave us is our free will.

My stepdads were allowed to make choices. My mom was free to make choices, and I too am free to make choices. While there were choices made that were heartbreaking for Him, they did not catch Him off guard.

Hebrews 4:13 says that nothing is hidden from God, and Psalm 24:1 says that the whole earth and everything in it belong to the Lord. In His sovereignty, He sees and is aware of and is over it all. But we still have our free will, and I believe it is all for the sake of love. If God had built inside us an inability to make any choices for ourselves, what other choice could we possibly have but to love Him? I think that God, like us, wants to be chosen. I think He wants a people who will choose Him above everything else and love Him out of their own free will. This is why even when bad choices are made, He is already putting a plan into action to reunite us with Him and His love.

Before He knit me in my mother's womb, God knew me and set a plan into motion to rewrite my story. He saw the pain before I felt it and had a plan to bring me comfort before one tear was ever shed. I love that the story is still a mystery to me. I have not planned every choice I will make in my life. But I am confident I can trust God to reveal His beauty and sovereignty throughout all my days.

I've often wondered about whether I can truly make a fatal mistake—a mistake that would actually mess up God's story for my life. I know I am not perfect and am capable of making mistakes, but if God is sovereign, knows the choices I will make, and is always working all things together for my good, can I truly end up at the wrong spot?

I really believe that when your life is fully surrendered to Jesus, His love surrounds you and provides that bumper to help steer you in the right direction. The bumper could be the people in your church family or community who notice you haven't quite been yourself or are making poor choices. They might call you out on it or take you to coffee and want to dig into your life and find out what's going on.

The bumper could also be in an encounter with Holy Spirit. It could happen in a moment you least expect it—while driving in your car, listening to music—and God just shows up and changes the whole atmosphere. I've definitely made choices in my life that led me down a detour and probably prolonged the journey to my destination, but I always ended up where I needed to be.

The more I live in this confidence, the less I find that fear has power to dominate my life. It may make an appearance in my life from time to time, tempting me to believe its lies again, but my heart and my spirit know better. Every time I face and defeat fear, it is smaller and easier to dismiss when it comes back. To know that I am deeply loved by my Father and that He is aligning my steps along the way puts my heart at rest and peace.

One of my favorite verses is Proverbs 16:9: "In their hearts humans plan their course, but the LORD establishes their steps." I can make plans and decisions all day long, but I have surrendered my life to Jesus over and over again. I belong to Him, and He cares deeply about what is His. I may have pain and heartbreak, and my path may not always be easy, but I know and I trust that He leads me back to Him every single time and that He will never abandon me.

When I consider the people in my past who caused me pain, I look at them again through the new eyes God gave me. It's like looking at the world with His perspective, which is so much greater than my own. I can feel His great love for them.

I can sense His pain at their negative choices. And I can believe, because I know from my own experience, that He still has a plan for their lives. There is nobody who is too lost for God, nobody who is unseen by Him. There is not a single person who has made such horrible choices that God will remove His love from them. He loves us in the middle of our mess and bad choices, and He loves us even when we reject Him.

It was so profound for me, all those years ago, in my greatest moment of integration healing to shout at Jesus that I hated Him and then to turn into a pile of mush as He responded with nothing but love and kindness. I realized in that moment that there really is nothing I can do to stop Him from loving me. Even now, when I think about that, I feel overwhelmed by His humility and kindness.

This was the revelation that turned me upside down in a stunning and marvelous way. God does not exist within time like we do. He is the God who was and is and is to come. He is with us both right now and on into our future. Jesus is God who took on human flesh and went to the cross to die as the atonement for our sins so we would be forgiven and reconciled to the One who created us.

While Jesus was in the garden, praying before He went to the cross, I imagine He was considering what He was about to do and all He was about to take on. He became sin itself, taking on every single bad choice any of us would ever make. Because He was God, Jesus knew the outcome. He knew He was about to go through incredible, unspeakable pain, but He also knew He would conquer death and darkness forever.

He knew every heart that would be saved because of this act. Because He is God, He knew me. In the same moment He was going to the cross, Jesus, who does not exist within time like us, was also with me in the very moment I was shouting at Him, "I hate you!" And He still chose to go to the cross and die for me. It wrecks me. I cannot fathom the strength and courage it took for Him to choose the cross, even in the face of outright hatred, rejection, and denial. This is the radical, undeniable, life-changing love of God that cannot be stopped or taken away.

This is the same love George loved me with. I think George was so full of the love of Jesus that it just came spilling out of him and onto me and my family. I rejected him over and over, and he never stopped loving me, telling me he loved me, taking care of me, and pursuing my heart. He was an example of Jesus to me before I could even realize it. I can't hold back the fountain of tears every time I think of this.

I want to be like George—so full of the love of God that I pour out nothing but love on those who want to reject me. In my human condition, I am not capable of conjuring up this love on my own. I need the love of Jesus to love others with. I can love those who hurt me because I have the love of God inside me. I am not made of steel—I can still feel pain and hurt and have my heart broken—but I can also keep my heart soft and vulnerable because of the love of God. I may encounter a storm and become afraid when I see the size of the waves, but I can trust in God because He has proven His sovereignty in my life again and again. I can forgive because He forgave me of so much. And I will surrender every single time, as many times as it takes, in order to keep giving myself to Jesus and living my life with Him, hand in hand.

This is why I worship. He is so worthy and has proven Himself every time to be so deserving of all that I can offer

Him. I sing even when it hurts. I shout His praise even when I struggle to believe He is good. I bring Him my heart even when I'm afraid and can't see what's ahead. And I sound like a blubbering weirdo when I'm trying to convey His love to a room full of people because I desperately do not want them to miss out on it. I would relive that awkward "How He Loves" moment a million times if it meant that more people would encounter His love. When you encounter the love of God, you can never be the same again.

A question I get asked at least twice a month is, "Kim, why do you laugh when you sing?" It's there on many of our recordings. You can hear me singing and then suddenly a giggle comes bursting through. Over the years, many have tried to duplicate it. It has been a hot topic of interviews.

There are a few reasons I might laugh during worship, but the main reason—and the most important—is simply that I am so deliriously happy. I am overcome with joy when I worship Jesus. When I worship Him, I can't help but think about what He saved me from and where He brought me from—and gratitude comes rushing in, filling my spirit, soul, and body up from the tips of my toes until it bubbles out of my mouth in laughter.

I am so happy He saved me. I have no idea what is coming next, what kind of mountains I will face or challenges I'll take on, but one thing is certain: I will worship Him for the rest of my life with every ounce of my being and with every breath I take, because He loves me.

ACKNOWLEDGMENTS

Thank you, Esther and Whitney, for believing in me and helping me make this dream come true. Thank you, Stephanie and the entire Zondervan team, for your hard work and dedication to this book. Thank you, Banning and my Jesus Culture family, for always pushing me, supporting me, and loving me. Thank you, Lauren, Yari, and Davina, for being the best friends a gal can have and loving me despite my crazy life! Thank you, Allie, for helping me tell this story. You coached me through the whole thing, encouraged me, and taught me so much. You are a dear friend, and I love you!

Skyler, you are the reason I can do all these things. You always push me, encourage me, and believe in me. You have loved me through many hard seasons, and I will forever be the lucky one. I love you!